THE SANDMAN™

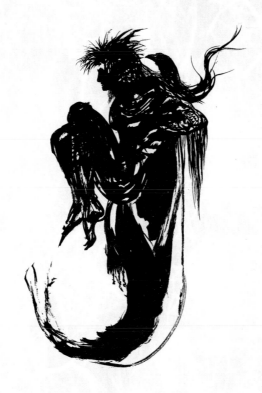

NEIL GAIMAN

Born in 1960 in Portchester, England, Neil Gaiman has written quite a lot of things.

His longest work to date is the ten volumes that comprise SANDMAN, which has won major awards in Austria, Brazil, England, Finland, Germany, Italy, Norway, Spain and the United States and several other countries he can't think of offhand.

His novels include *Neverwhere* (which began life as a TV series, and is soon to be a major motion picture, because nothing is ever soon to be a minor motion picture), and STARDUST (which won the Mythopoeic Award as best fantasy novel of 1999, and is available in illustrated and unillustrated versions).

Many of his short stories have been collected in *Smoke and Mirrors: Short Stories and Illusions*. Of his shorter comics works, he is proudest of MR. PUNCH. He is writing a new novel at present. It's called *American Gods*.

He has exactly three children, approximately seven cats, and a house that wants to be Gormenghast when it grows up.

He tends to need a haircut. Currently he needs a shave as well.

YOSHITAKA AMANO

Moving fluidly from medium to medium and style to style, Yoshitaka Amano has established himself as one of Japan's premier — and most popular — artists.

As a member of the venerable animation company Tatsunoko Studios, Amano created memorable characters such as *G-Force* and *Hutch the HoneyBee*. Throughout his career, he has also published over 17 illustrated fantasy books, including the cult classic *Vampire Hunter D*. His innovative character designs and illustrations cross over into video games as well, with his work appearing in the wildly popular interactive role playing game series *Final Fantasy*. In 1997 he collaborated with the Los Angeles Philharmonic to create *1,001 Nights*, an animated film/music project. His other artistic outlets include printmaking, scenic design, and stained glass. THE SANDMAN: THE DREAM HUNTERS is Amano's American comics debut.

In October 1999, Amano mounted his second major American exhibition, a multimedia event entitled *Hero*. Held at the Angel Orensanz Foundation in New York City, the *Hero* Exhibition was the first of a series of projects about a reincarnated prince on an epic quest ten thousand years in the future. The exhibition also featured original artwork from THE DREAM HUNTERS.

DC COMICS ❧ Jenette Kahn, President & Editor-in-Chief ❧ Paul Levitz, Executive Vice President & Publisher ❧ Karen Berger, Executive Editor ❧ Jennifer Lee, Assistant Editor ❧ Georg Brewer VP-Design & Retail Product Development ❧ Amie Brockway-Metcalf Art Director ❧ Richard Bruning VP-Creative Director ❧ Patrick Caldon Senior VP-Finance & Operations ❧ Dorothy Crouch VP-Licensed Publishing ❧ Terri Cunningham VP-Managing Editor ❧ Joel Ehrlich Senior VP-Advertising & Promotions ❧ Alison Gill VP-Manufacturing ❧ Lillian Laserson VP & General Counsel ❧ Jim Lee Editorial Director-WildStorm ❧ David McKillips VP-Advertising ❧ John Nee VP & General Manager-WildStorm ❧ Cheryl Rubin VP-Licensing & Merchandising ❧ Bob Wayne VP-Sales & Marketing

The Dream Hunters Logo Design ❧ Nancy Ogami

VERTIGO
DC COMICS

Second Printing
ISBN: 1-56389-629-X

THE SANDMAN™

The Dream Hunters

written by

NEIL GAIMAN

illustrated by

YOSHITAKA AMANO

Chapter one

A monk lived in solitude beside a temple on the side of a mountain. It was a small temple, and the monk was a young monk, and the mountain was not the most beautiful or impressive mountain in Japan.

The monk tended the temple, and he passed his days in peace and quiet until the day that a fox and a badger passed the temple and spied the monk hoeing the little plot of yams which fed him for much of the year.

The badger looked at the monk and the temple, and he said, "Let us make a wager. Whichever of us succeeds in driving that man from the temple will keep the place as a home; for it has been many years since pilgrims or travellers came to this temple, and it will be a finer place by far to live than a badger's set or a fox's den."

And the fox smiled with her sharp teeth, and blinked her green eyes, and she swished her brush and she looked down the hill at the temple and at the monk, then she looked at the badger and she said, "Very well. A wager it is."

"Each of us will take it in turns," said the badger. "I shall go first."

Down in his little garden plot the monk hoed his yams, then he went down on his knees and he weeded the wild onions and the ginger plants and the little patch of herbs: then he cleaned the mud from his hands and knees, and he went into the living quarters at the back of the temple, to prepare for that evening's devotions.

That night, the moon hung full, huge and silver, in a night sky the colour of a ripe plum; and the priest heard a mighty commotion outside his door.

There were five men in the courtyard, richly dressed and mounted on five great horses. They were hairy men. Their leader held a great curved sword.

"Who serves in this temple?" he called, in a voice like the thunder. "Let him show himself!"

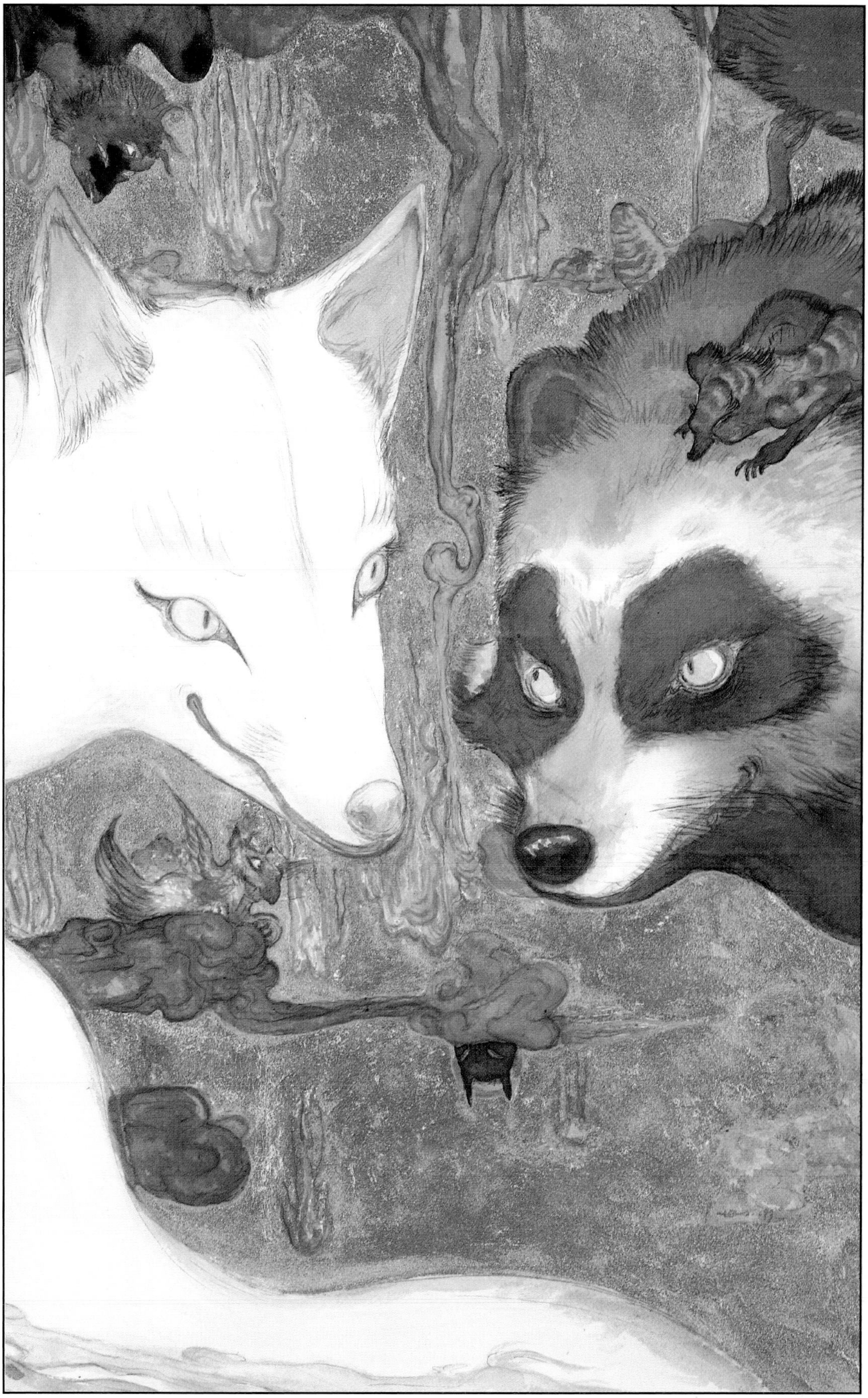

The monk came forward, into the moonlight, and he bowed deeply. "I am the unworthy guardian of this temple," he said, simply.

"And a skinny, unimpressive runt of a priest you are," boomed the leader. "But who among us can account for the will of the gods? Truly was it said that those who seek after fortune find it as elusive as grasping a rainbow, while those who disdain good fortune and the world often find it beating upon a gong outside their door."

To this speech the young monk said nothing, but he raised his head a little, and he looked at the horsemen in the moonlight with sharp eyes that missed nothing at all.

"Well, do you wish to know what your good fortune is?"

"Certainly," said the monk.

"Know then that you have been sent for by none other than the Emperor himself. You are to travel as fast as you can to the Imperial Palace, where the Emperor wishes to speak with you and to confirm that you are indeed the person of whom the augurs and diviners have told him, and then you will be raised from obscurity and appointed to minister to the needs of the imperial court — a position which brings with it great fortune and mighty estates.

"However, know also that if you do not present yourself at the Imperial Palace before the next Day of the Monkey, then the auguries go from good to very bad, and the Emperor shall, regretfully, be forced to issue your death warrant. Therefore wait not a single moment, but depart this place before dawn, or risk the Emperor's severest displeasure."

The horses stamped their feet in the full moon's light.

The monk bowed low once more.

"I shall leave instantly," he said, and the five horsemen grinned, the moonlight gleaming from their eyes and their teeth, and from the metal bridles and decorations of their horses, "but, before I leave, I have one question to ask."

"And what would that be?" asked the leader, in a voice like a tiger's roar.

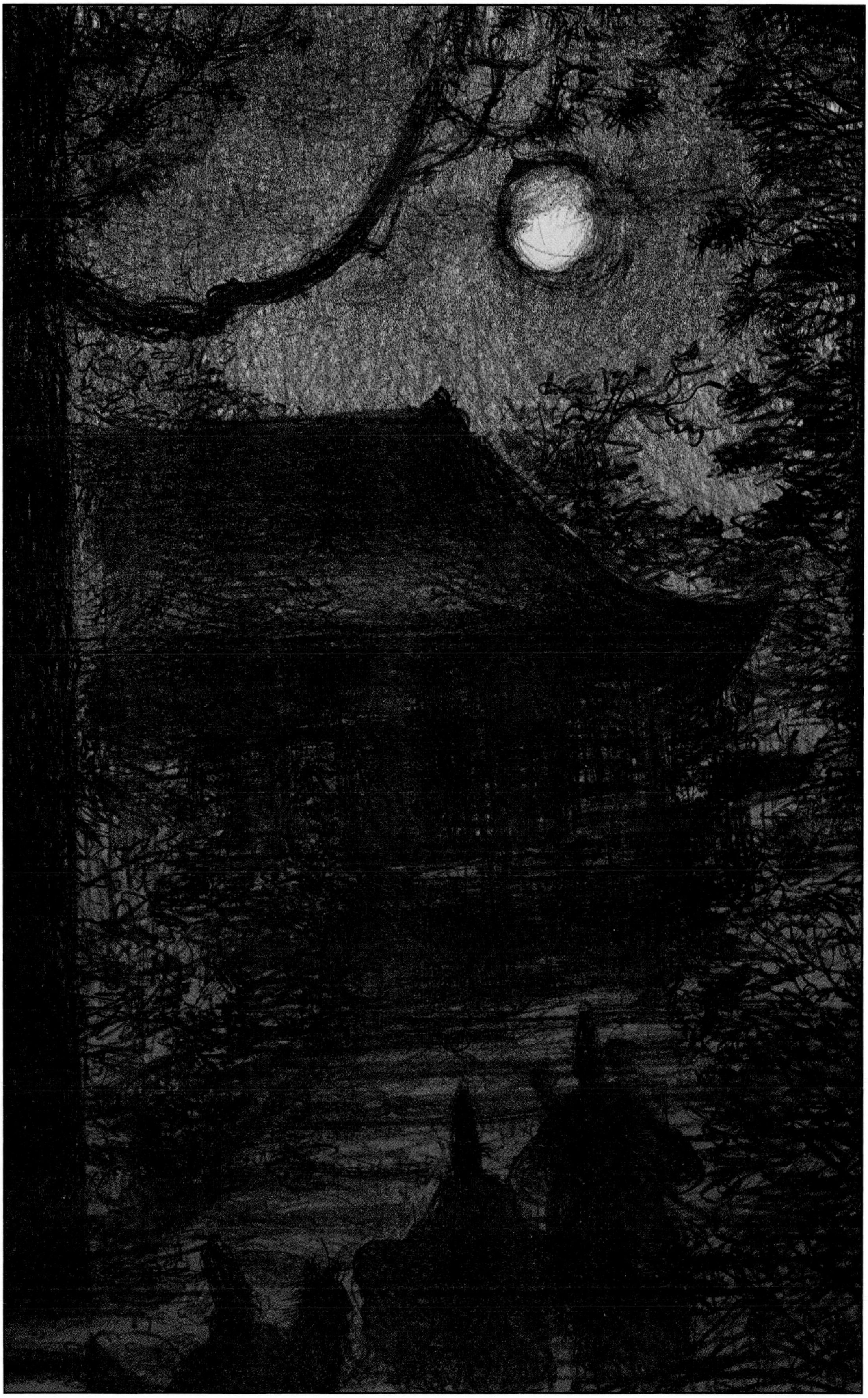

"Why the Emperor would send a badger to tell me to come to the Imperial Court," said the monk, who had observed that, while the first four horses had the tails of horses, the last horse of all had the tail of a badger. And with that the monk began to laugh, and he walked back into the temple to begin his evening devotions.

There was a clattering from the courtyard as the riders rode away, and from the mountainside came the *yip! yip! yip!* of a fox, high and vicious and amused.

The clouds covered the mountaintop before midday the next day, and they were dark, full clouds, so it came as no surprise to the monk when the rain began to fall, a hard, drenching rain that bent the bamboo and flattened the young yam plants. The monk, who was used to the weather on the side of the mountain, remained at his devotions and did not stir, not even when the lightning started — a blinding whiteness, followed by thunder so loud and so deep it felt as if it were being wrenched from the very heart of the mountain.

The rain redoubled. It sounded like the beating of a hundred small drums, such that the monk could scarcely hear the sound of weeping, over the pounding and rattling of the rain, but he did hear someone sobbing, and he went out into the courtyard, where he saw, sprawled upon the ground where the earth ran like muddy soup, a young woman, soaked by the rain. Her robes, which were of the richest silk, were sopping, and clung to her body like a second skin.

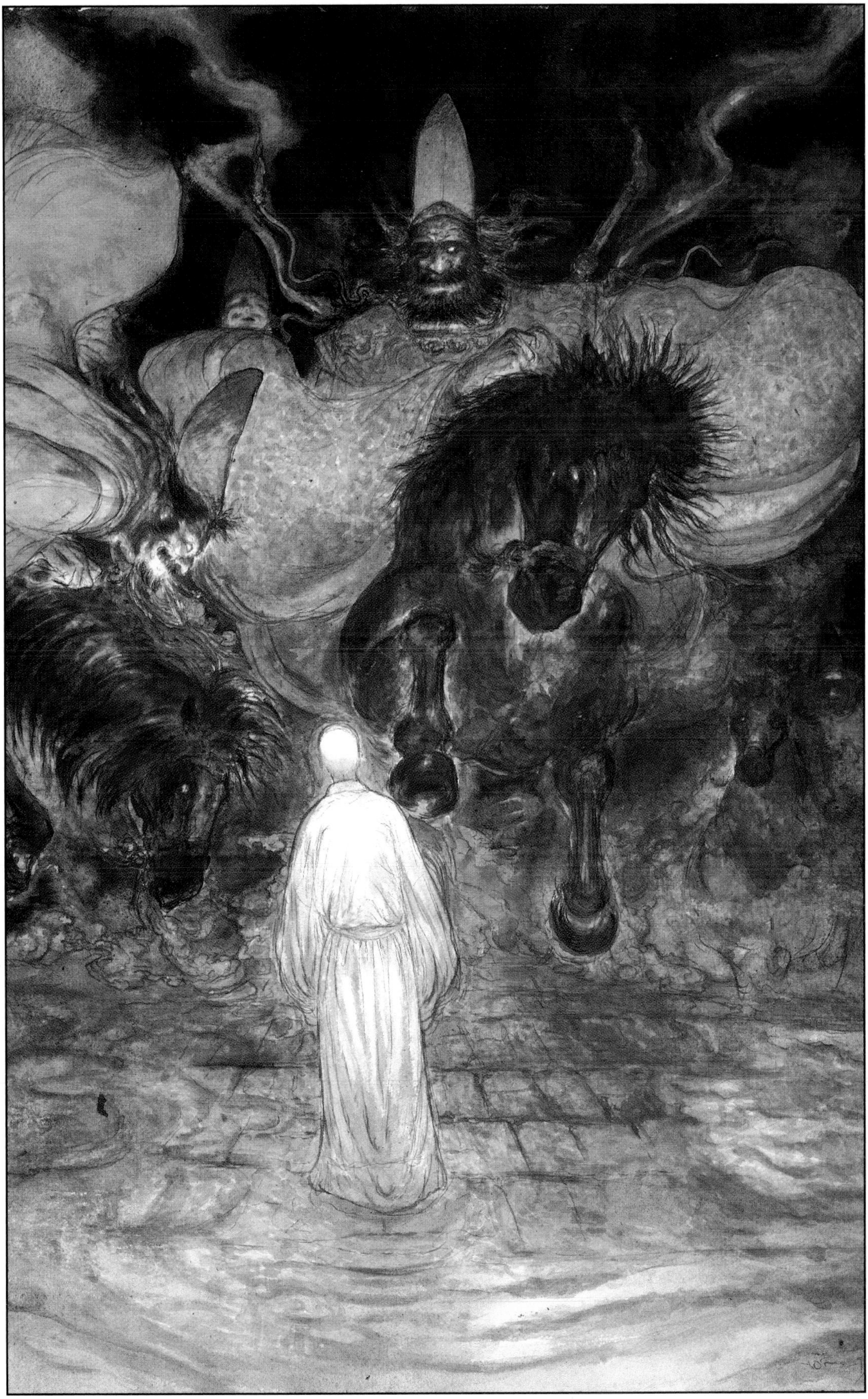

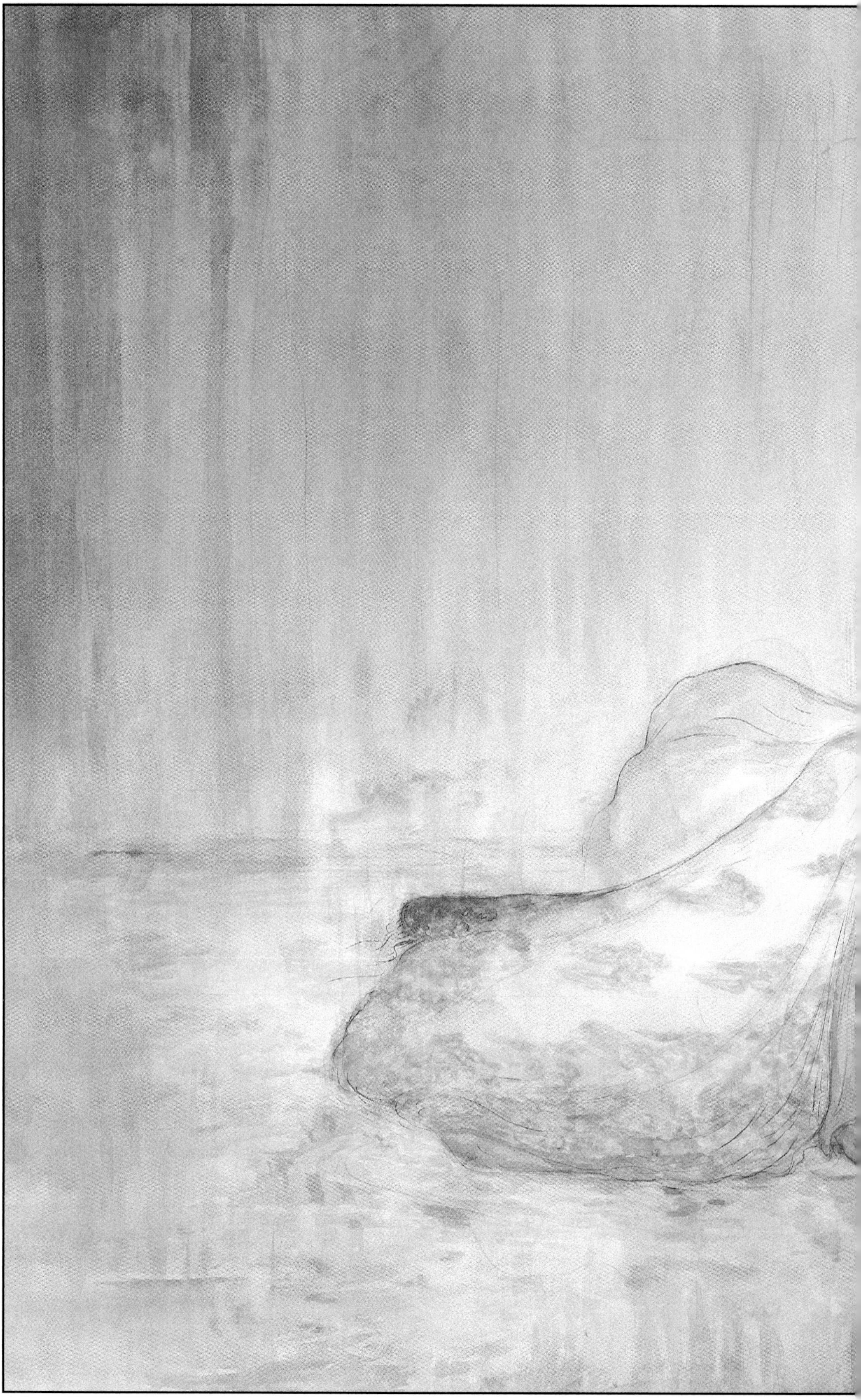

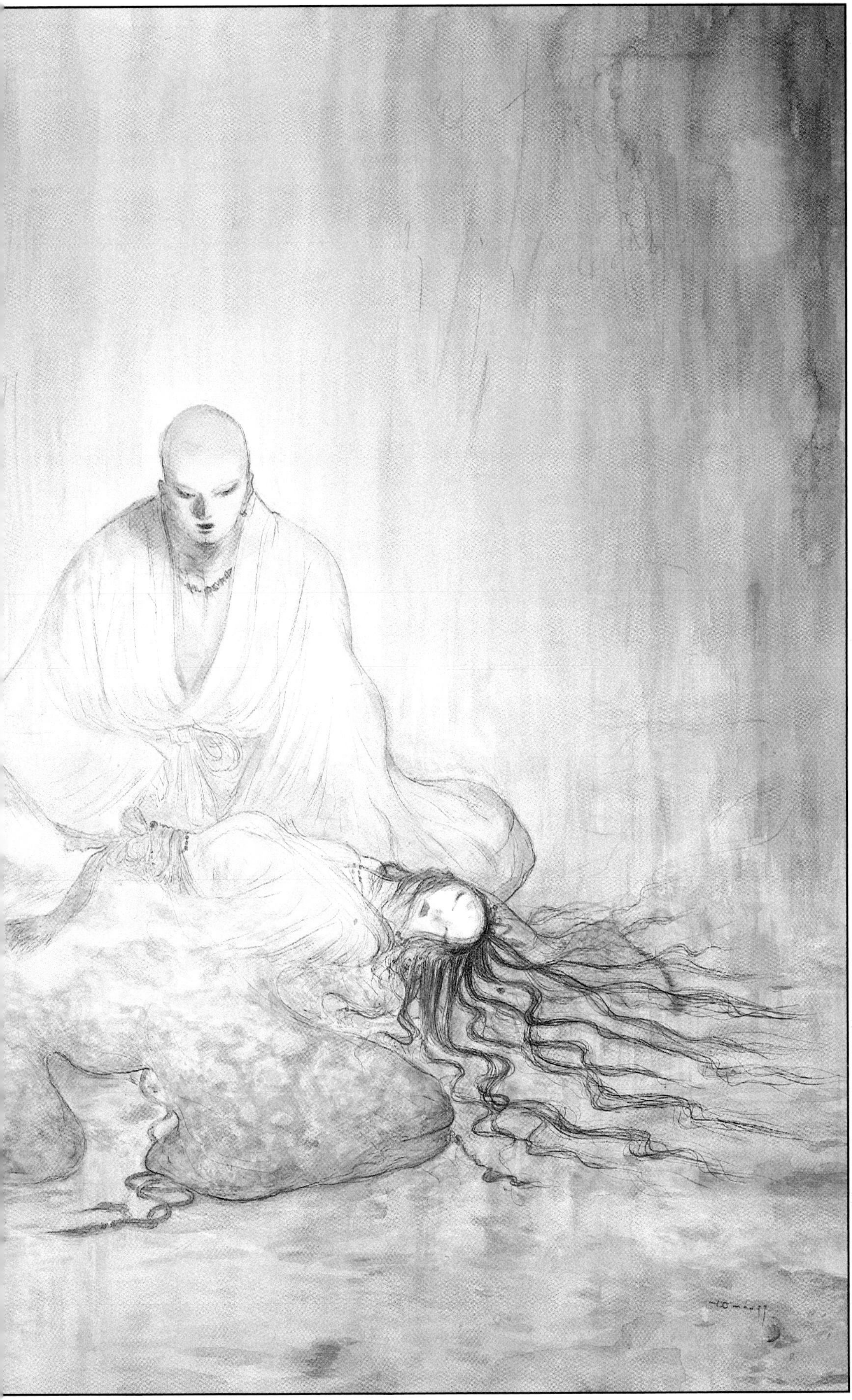

The monk was painfully aware of the young woman's beauty, and her body, as he helped her to her feet and walked beside her into the temple, where they could be out of the rain.

"I am the only daughter of the governor of the province of Yamashiro," she told him, as she stood beside the small brazier, wringing out her garments and her long black hair, "and I was travelling with a party of women and guards to this very temple, when we were attacked by brigands. I alone escaped. I overheard them say that, when this rain lets up they are going to ride up the mountainside to this temple and burn it to the ground and kill anyone they find here." While she spoke she ate a bowl of the monk's rice, and a small bowl of yams, gobbling her food hungrily as she stared at the monk with bright green eyes.

"Therefore," she said, "let us flee this place, never to return, before the bandits come, for if we stay here, we shall both perish. And if we are separated, then you should make your way to the province of Yamashiro, and ask for my father, who is the governor, and has the finest house in the province, and he will reward you mightily. Thank you for the rice. It was very good, although the yams were perhaps a little dry."

"We must certainly leave immediately," said the monk, with a gentle smile playing at the corners of his lips, "if you will explain one thing to me first."

"And what would that be?" asked the girl.

"Explain to me how it happens that the daughter of the governor of the province of Yamashiro happens to be a fox," said the monk, "for I have never seen eyes like yours on a human face."

At that, no quicker than it takes to tell it, the girl jumped over the little brazier, and, when she landed she was no longer a girl but a fox, with its coat sleek and its brush held high, and it darted the monk a look of utter disdain before it leapt upon a stone wall and ran along it, to the shade of a bent old pine, where it paused for a moment, before vanishing into the storm.

Later that afternoon the sun came out, and the monk was able to walk around the temple picking up blown leaves and fallen branches, and repairing the damage of the storm.

He was beginning to perceive a pattern here.

So he was not entirely surprised when, several nights later, as the sun was setting, a troop of demons shambled through the woods to surround the little temple. Some of them had the heads of dead men, and some of them had the heads of monsters, with yellow tusks and staring eyes and huge horns; and they set up a clamor such that you have never heard.

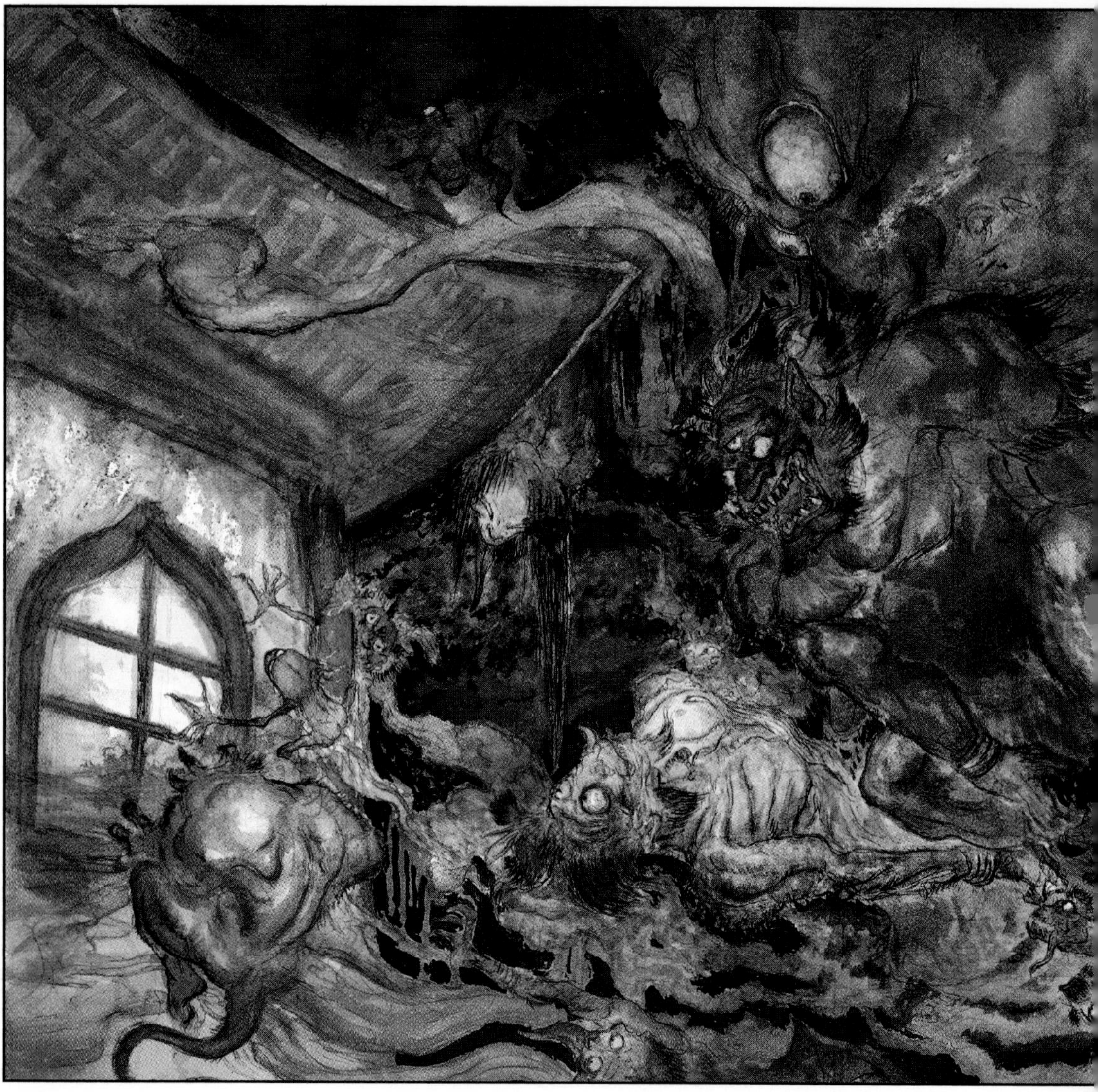

"We smell a man!" they shouted. "We scent man-flesh! Bring out the man and we shall eat him — we shall roast his heart and vitals and brains, feast on his eyes and his cheeks and his tongue, swallow his liver and his fat and his testicles! Bring him here!"

And with that, several of the demons began to pile high the fallen branches the monk had gathered, and they breathed on them with their fiery breath until the branches began to smoke and then to burn.

"And if I do not come out?" called the monk.

"Then we shall come back every night at sundown," screamed a demon with a head like a flayed bat, "and make a tumult, until, finally, our patience at an end, we shall burn down your little temple and we shall pluck your charred body from the ashes, and chomp it down eagerly with our sharp teeth!"

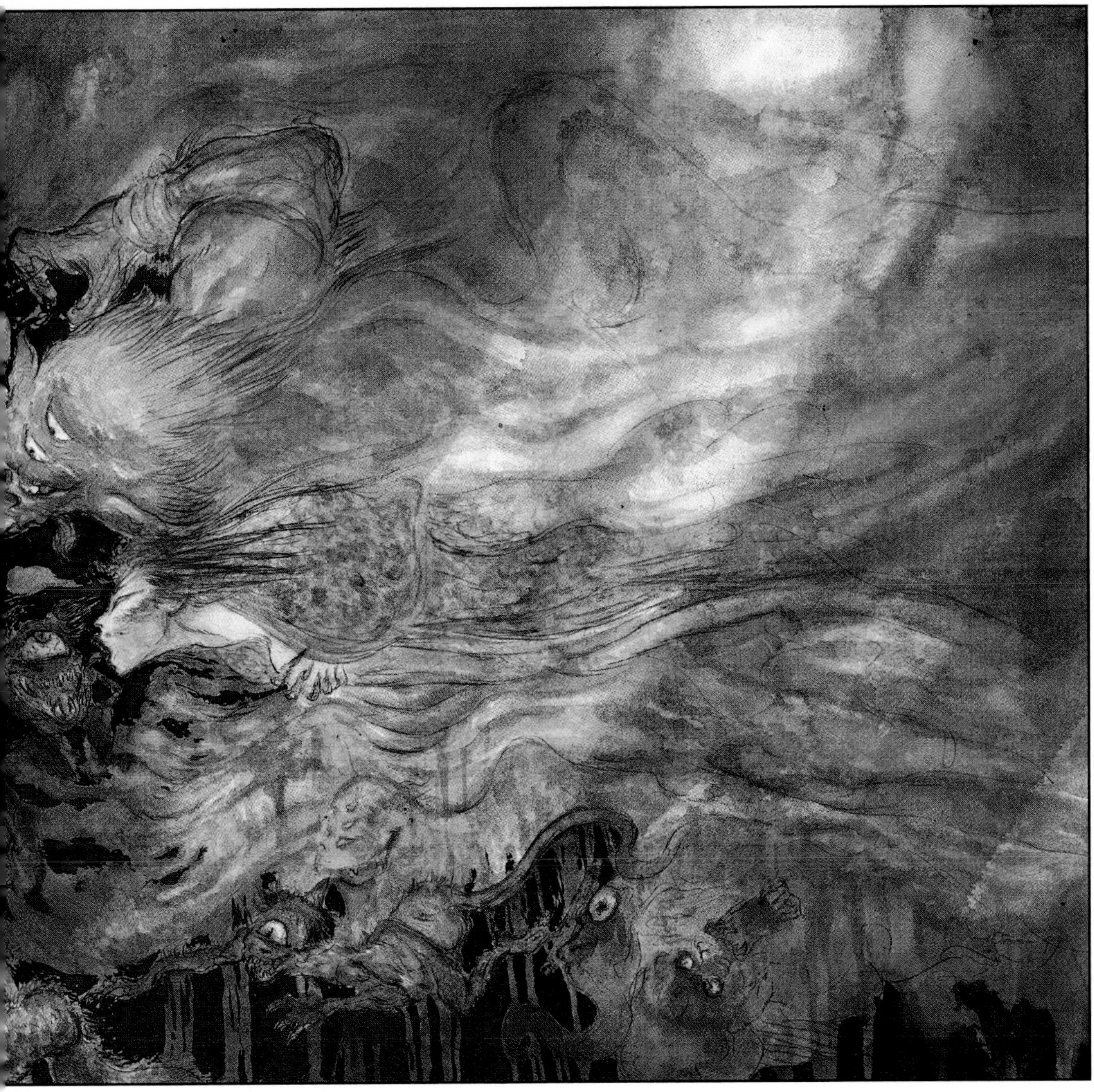

"So flee!" shouted another demon, its face that of a drowned man, flesh swollen, eyes blind and pearl-like, "flee this place and never come back!"

But the monk did not flee. Instead he walked out into the courtyard, and he picked up a burning brand from the fire.

"I will not leave this place," he said, "and I am tired of these performances. Now, whatever you are, fox or badger, take that! And that!" and he began to lay about him with the burning brand.

In a moment, where before there had stood a horde of demons, there was nothing more than a fat old he-badger, who scrabbled and began to run away. The monk threw the burning brand at the badger and struck him on the rear, burning its tail-fur and singeing its rump. The badger howled with pain, and vanished into the night.

At dawn the monk was half-woken from his sleep by a whispering voice from behind him.

"I wished to say sorry," said the voice. "It was a wager between the badger and me."

The monk said nothing.

"The badger has fled to another province, his tail burned and his dignity in shreds," said the girl's voice. "I shall also leave, if you desire it. But I have lived my life in a den above the waterfall, by the twisted pine, and it would hurt me to leave."

"Then stay," said the monk, "if you will play no more of your foolish fox tricks upon me."

"Of course," said the whispering girl's voice behind him, and soon the monk returned to dreams. When he woke properly, an hour later, the monk found fox-footprints on the matting of his room.

The monk caught sight of the fox from time to time, slipping through the undergrowth, and the sight of her always made him smile.

He did not know that the fox had fallen violently in love with him, when she came to tell him she was sorry, or perhaps before, when he had picked her up from the muddy courtyard and taken her inside to dry herself by the fire. But whenever it had happened, it was unquestionably true that the fox was in love with the young monk.

And that was to be the cause of much misery in the time to come. Much misery, and heartbreak, and of a strange journey.

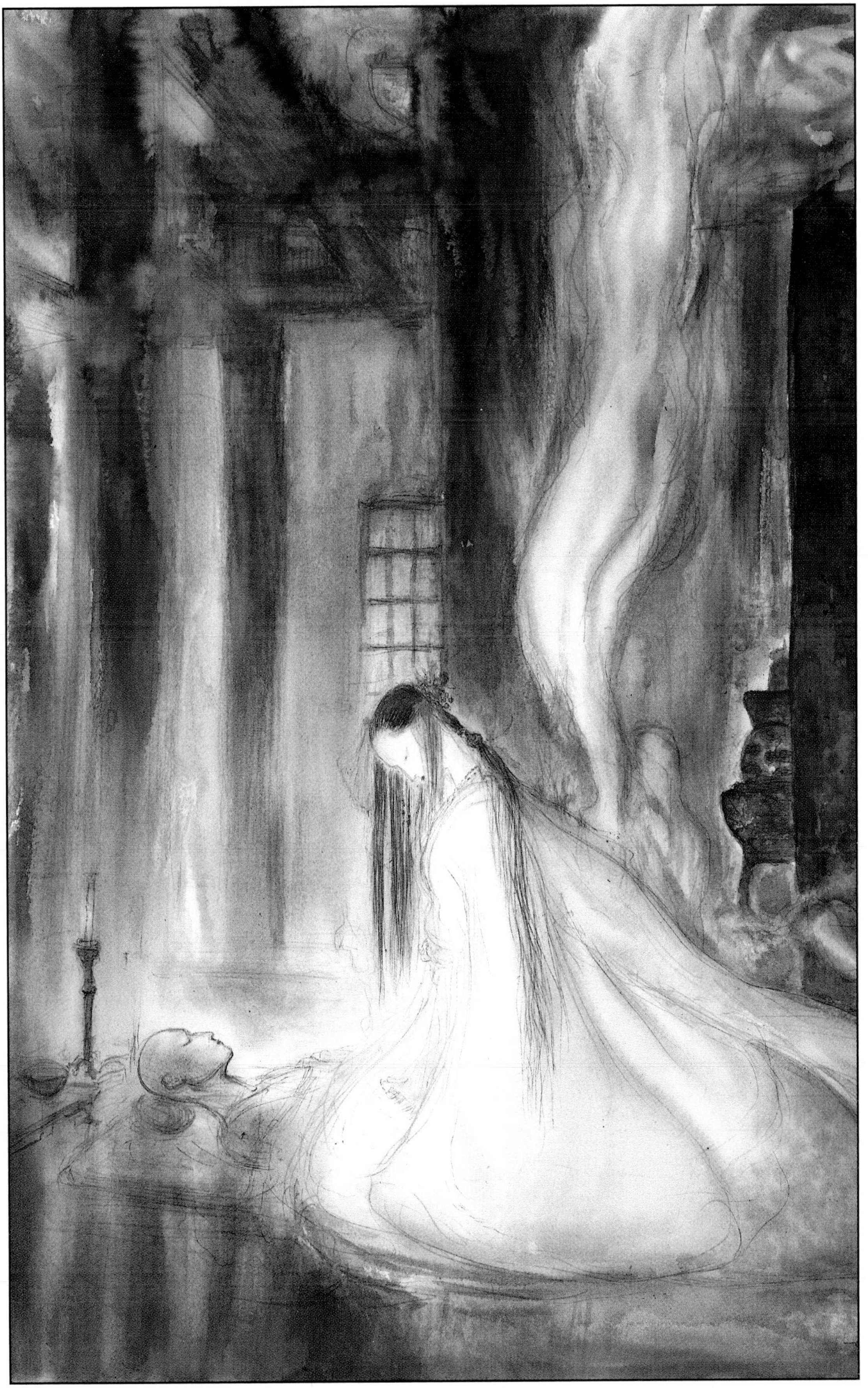

Chapter two

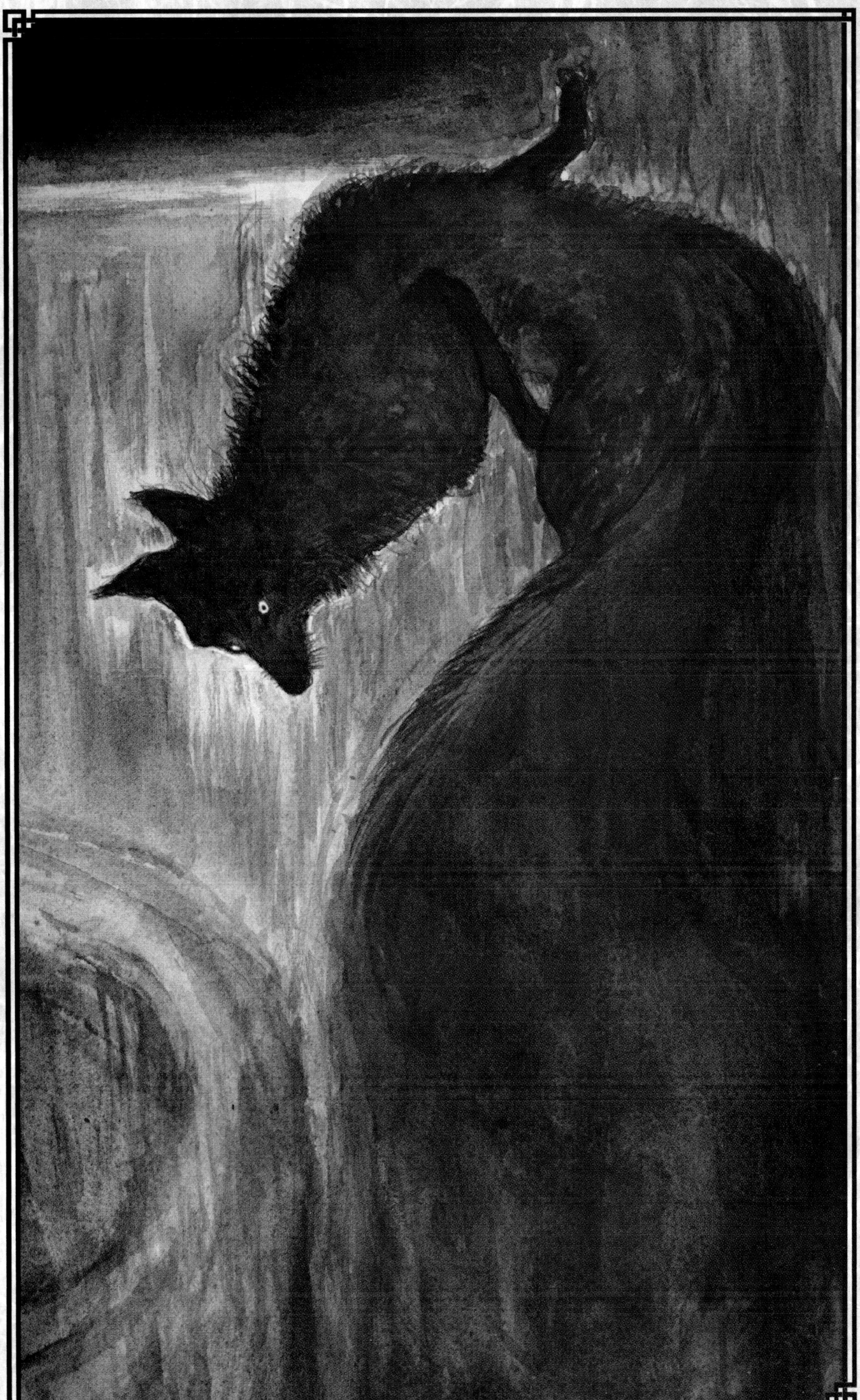

Now in those days there were many things walking the earth that we rarely see today. There were ghosts and demons, and spirits of all kinds; there were beast gods and little gods and great gods; there were all manner of entities, beings, and wraiths and creatures, both kind and malevolent.

The fox was hunting on the mountainside one night, after the moon had set and the night was at its darkest, when she saw, by a blasted pine tree, several bluish lights glimmering. Quiet and quick as a shadow she slipped toward them. As she approached, the lights resolved themselves into strange creatures, neither alive nor dead, which glowed with the flickering blue of marsh gas.

The creatures were talking to each other in low voices.

"So we are commanded," said the first creature, blue flame glistening on its naked skin, "and the monk shall die."

The fox stopped moving then, and concealed herself behind a clump of ferns.

"Aye," said the second, its teeth sharp as tiny knives. "Our master, who is a Yin-Yang Diviner of great power, from his studies of the stars and of the patterns of the earth, has seen that, come the next full of the moon, either he or the monk shall be dead — and if it is not the monk, then it must be our master."

"How, then, shall he die?" asked the third creature, its eyes shining with blue flame. "Hush! Is there any thing listening to our counsel? For I feel eyes upon me."

The fox held her breath, and pushed her belly down into the earth, and lay still. The three creatures rose higher into the air and stared down at the dark woods. "There is nothing here but a dead fox," said the first creature.

A fly alighted on the fox's forehead, and walked, slowly, down to the tip of her muzzle. She resisted the urge to snap at it; instead she just lay there, eyes unfocused and blank, a dead thing.

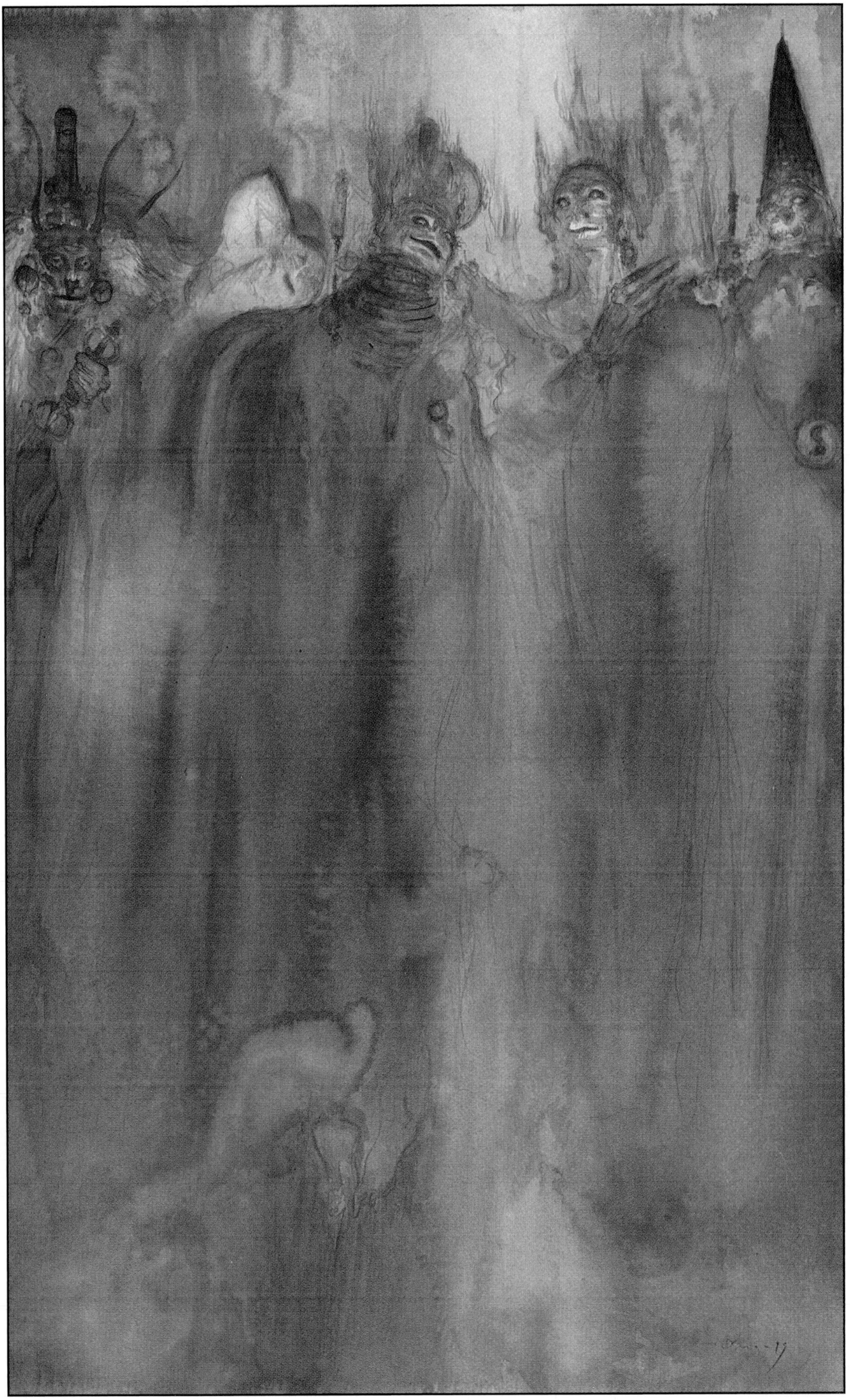

"This is what our master intends," said the first of the creatures. "For three nights running, the monk shall have evil dreams. On the first night the monk shall dream of a box. On the second night he shall dream of a black key. On the third night he shall dream that he unlocks the box with the key. When, in his dream, he opens the box, he shall lose all connection to this world, and without food, and without water, he will die soon enough. His death will not be held to our master's conscience." And then it looked about it one more time. "Can you be certain that we are not overheard?"

The fly crawled onto the fox's eyeball. She did not blink, although the tickling felt like madness in her mind.

"What could hear us?" asked the second of the creatures. "A fox's corpse?" And it laughed, high and distant.

"But it would not matter if someone did hear us," said the first of them, "for if someone did overhear us, and spoke of what he heard to another, no sooner would the first word leave his mouth than his heart will burst in his breast."

A cold wind blew over the mountaintop. The sky began to lighten in the east.

"But is there no way the monk can escape his fate?" said the third.

"Only one way," said the second.

The fox strained to hear another word, but there was nothing, no more words were spoken. All she could hear was the whisper of the wind as it stirred the fallen leaves, the sighing of the trees as they breathed and swayed in the wind, and the distant *ting ting* of wind chimes in the little temple.

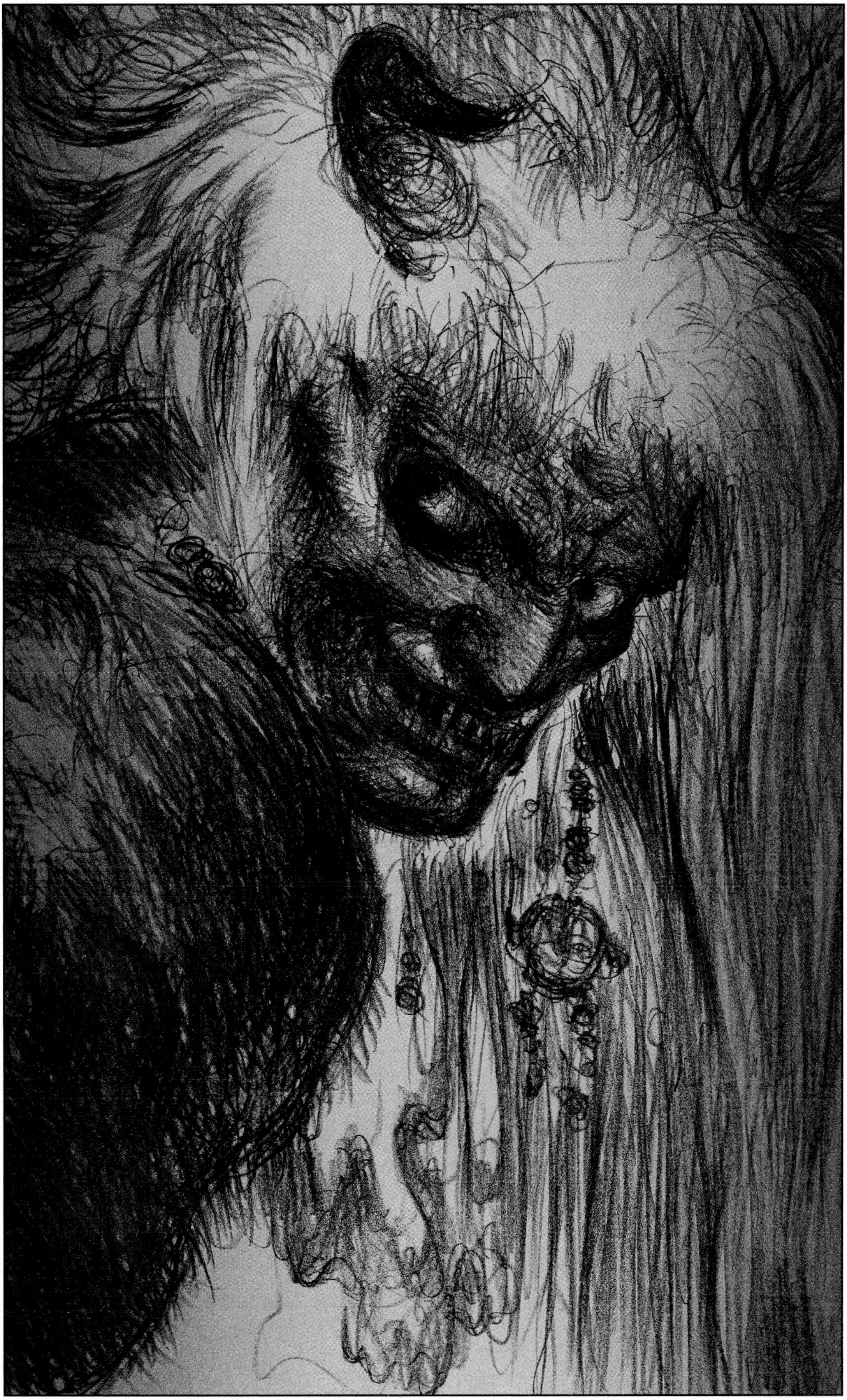

She lay there stiff as a fallen branch until the sun was high in the sky.
Then she swished her tail, and snapped at the ants who were crawling over
her paw; she made her way down the side of the mountain, until she reached
her den. It was cool in her den, and dark, and it smelled of earth, and in the
back of the fox's den was her most precious thing.

She had found it several years before, tangled in the roots of a great tree;
so she had dug, and chewed, and dug some more, for days, until she had it
out of the ground, and then she had licked it clean with her pink tongue,
and had polished it with her own fur, and she had taken it back to her den,
where she venerated it, and cared for it. It was her treasure. It was very old,
and it had come from a far country.

It was a carving of a dragon, carved from jade, and its eyes were
tiny red stones.

The dragon brought her comfort. In the gloom of her den its ruby eyes
glowed, casting a warm radiance.

The fox picked her treasure up in her mouth, carrying it as gently as she
would have carried one of her own kits.

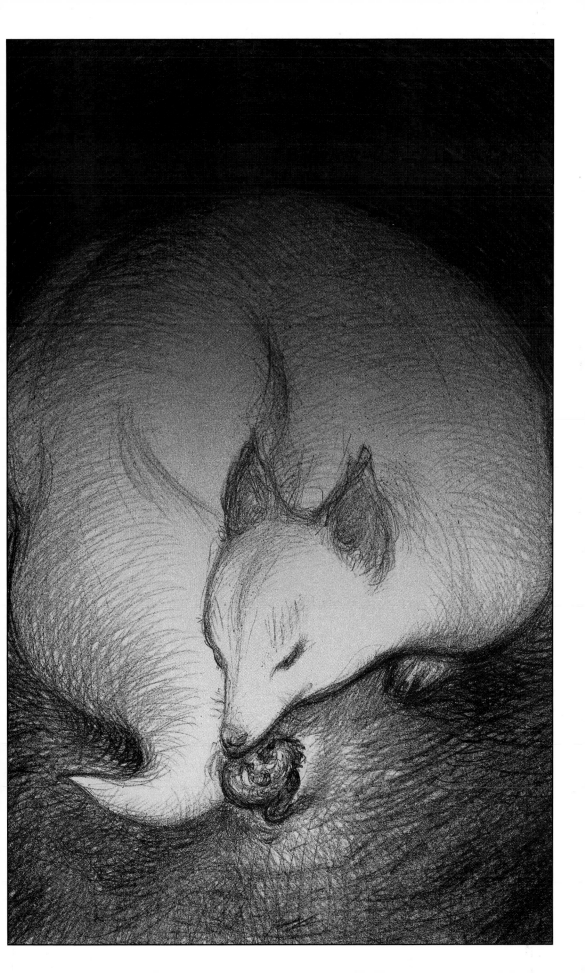

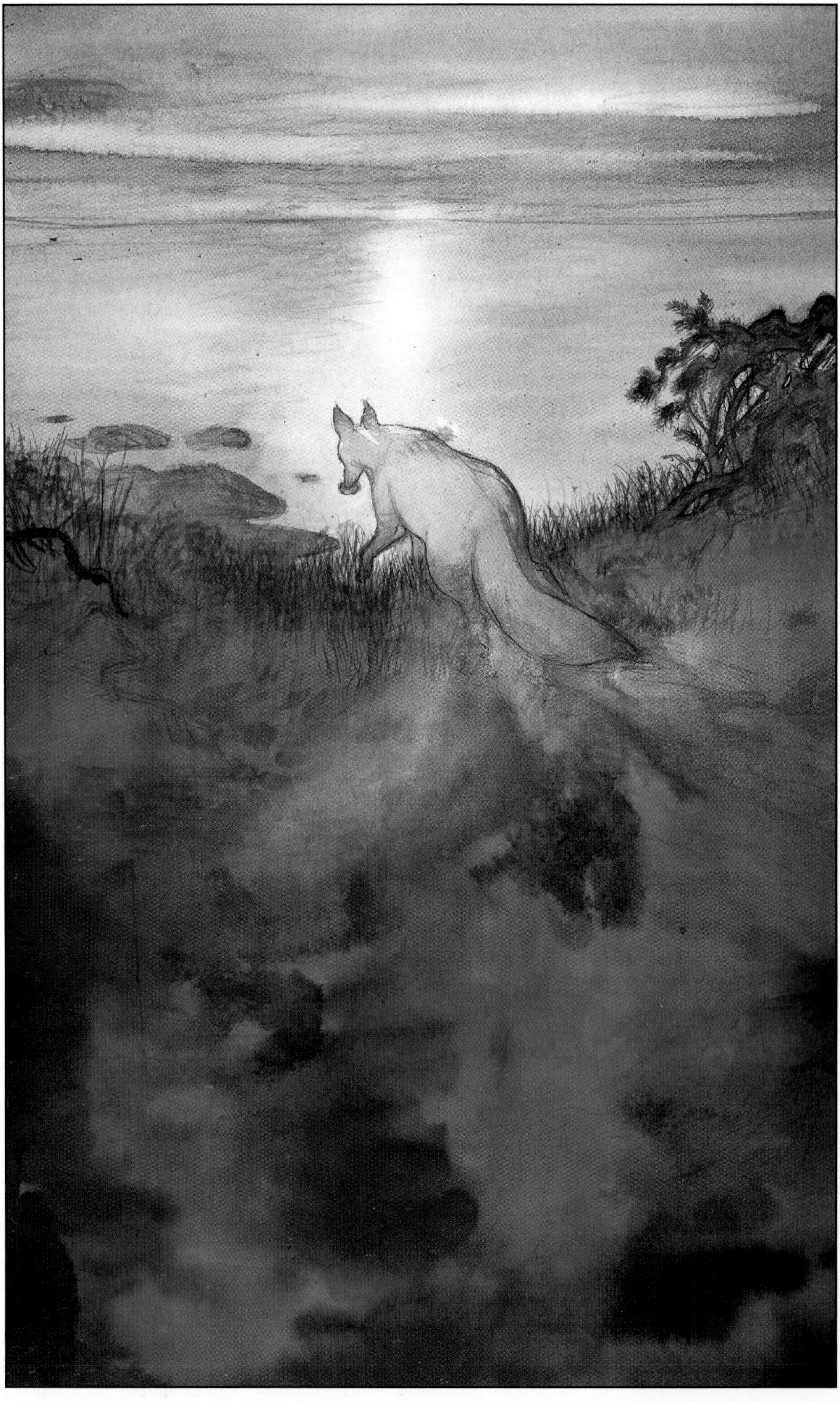

She carried the statue in her mouth for many miles, until she came to a cliff at the edge of the sea. She could hear the seagulls screaming above her, and the pounding of the cold waves on the rocks below her. She could taste the salt on the air.

"For this is my most precious possession," she thought. "And I give it up, give it to the sea, and all I ask is the knowledge of how to save the life of the monk. For if I do nothing he shall dream of a box, and then of a key, and then of a key opening the box, and then he will be dead."

And then she nuzzled the pale jade statue over the cliff-edge, gently, and watched it tumble hundreds of feet into the churning sea. Then she sighed, for the little statue of the dragon had brought serenity and peace to her den.

Then she walked the miles back to her den and, tired beyond all imagining, she slept.

This was the dream the fox dreamed.

She was in a barren place of grey rock and brown rock, where nothing grew. The sky was grey as well, neither light nor dark. Poised on a great rock in front of her was a huge fox, jet black from the tip of its muzzle to almost the end of its tail, which was as white as if it had been dipped into a paint-pot. It was bigger than a tiger, bigger than a war-horse, bigger than any creature the fox had ever seen.

It stood on the rock as if it were waiting for something, and its eyes were dark pits in which distant stars glinted and burned.

The fox clambered and sprang from rock to rock until she stood in front of the fox of dreams, and she prostrated herself in front of him, rolling over to show him her throat.

Stand, said the great fox. *Stand and have no fear. You gave up much to dream this dream, child.*

The fox got to her feet. In her dream she was not shaking, although she was more scared than any little fox has ever been.

"My dragon," she asked. "Was it yours, Lord?"

No, he told her. *But it was lost, long long ago, by one whom I called friend, back before the true dragons left this place to swim in the sky. My friend lost the statue, and it troubled him. Now the sea shall wash it back to him, and he will sleep more peacefully, at the bottom of the Great Deeps, with the rest of his kind, until the next age of the world.*

"I am honoured and grateful to have been permitted to be of service to your friend," said the fox.

They stood there in silence for some timeless moments, in the dream-place, the tiny fox and the great black fox. The little fox looked about the rocky waste.

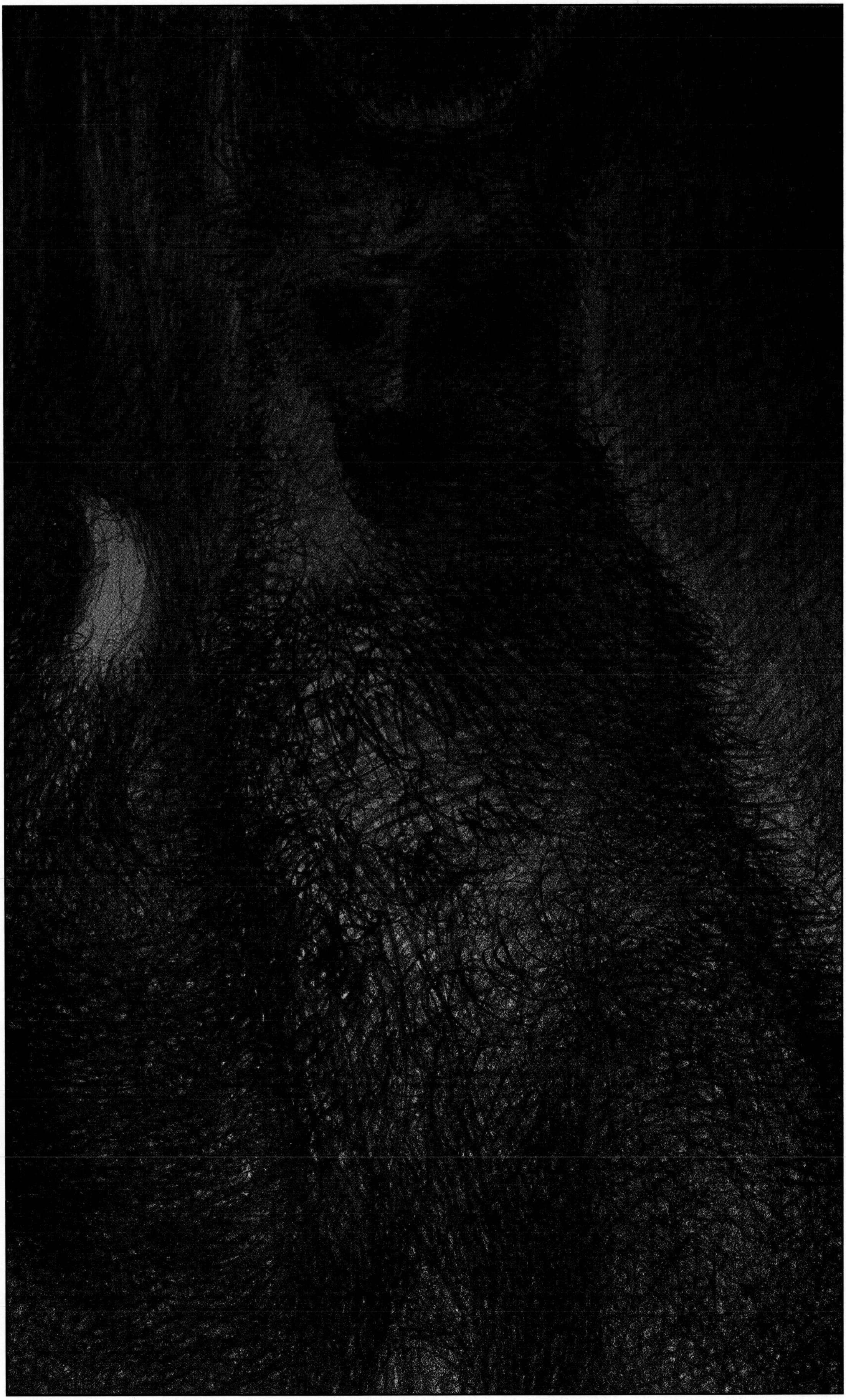

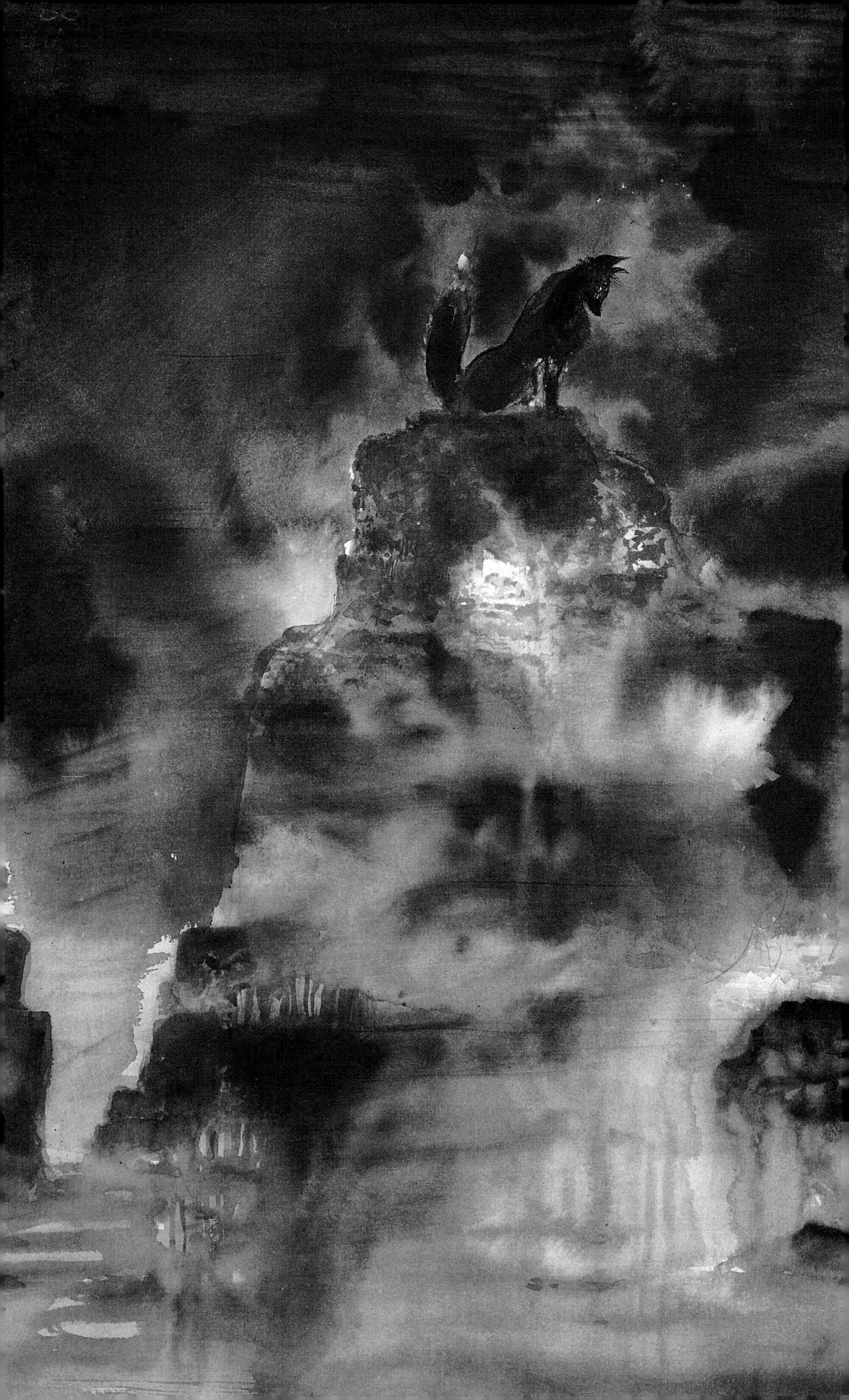

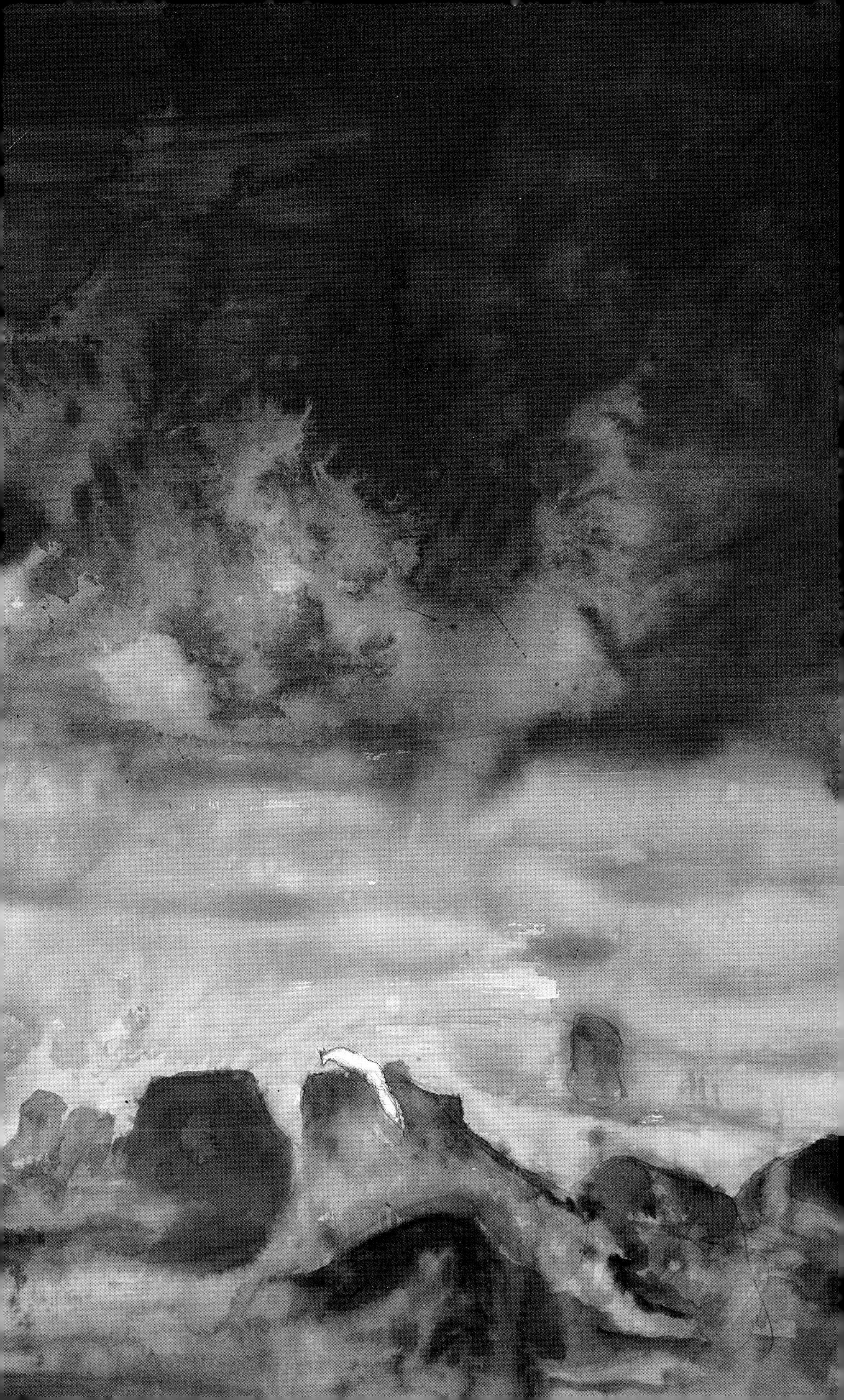

"What are those animals?" asked the little fox.

They were the size of lions, and they snuffled about the rocks, their long noses rooting and snuffling in the barren ground.

They are Baku, said the great fox. *They are the Dream Eaters.*

The little fox had heard of the Baku. If a dreamer wakes from a dream of ill-omen or a portent of dark things, the dreamer may invoke the Baku, and hope that the Baku will eat the dream, and take it and what it foretells, away.

She stared at the Baku, as they moved across the rocky desert of dreams.

"And if one were to catch a Baku after it had consumed a dream," asked the fox. "What then?"

The great fox said nothing for some time. In the hollow of an eye one distant star glittered. *Baku are hard to catch, and harder to hold. They are elusive and crafty beasts.*

"I am a fox," she said, humbly, and without boasting. "I also am a crafty beast."

The great fox nodded assent. Then he looked down at her, and it seemed to the fox that he could see everything she was, everything she dreamed, and hoped, and felt. *He is only a human,* said the great fox. *While you are a fox. These things rarely end happily.*

And the fox would have told him what she thought of this, and opened her heart to him, but with a flick of his tail the great fox leapt from the rock down to the desert floor below. And it seemed to the fox that he grew and he grew, until he was the size of the sky, and the huge fox was the night, and stars twinkled in the blackness of his coat, and the white tip of his tail was the half-moon, shining in the night sky.

"I can be crafty," said the little fox to the night. "And I can be brave. And I would die for him."

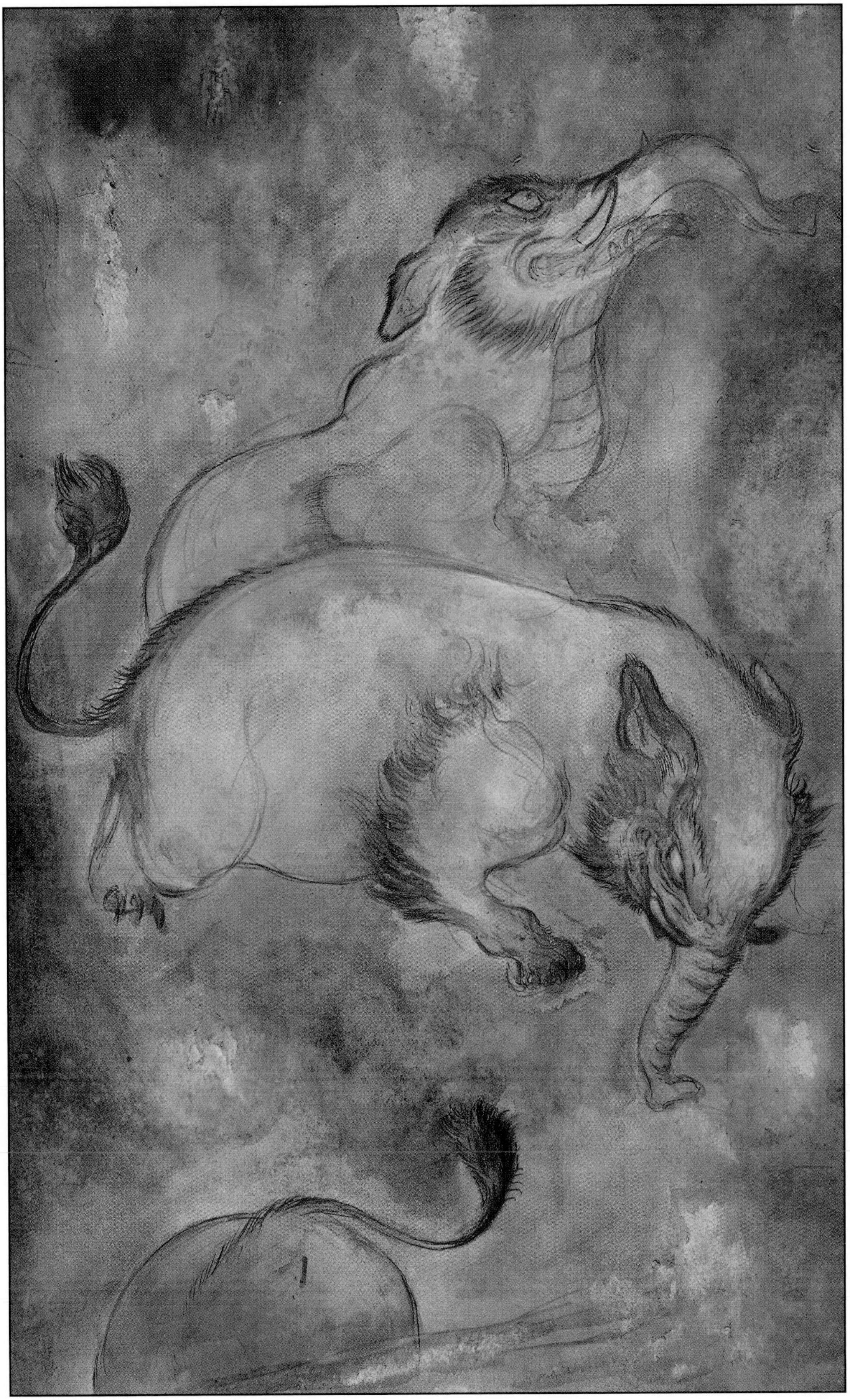

And the fox imagined that a voice in her head was saying, almost tenderly, *Then catch his dreams, child*, as she awoke.

The sun was the golden of the late afternoon, and it burnished the world as the fox stepped into the brush and made for the little temple, stopping only to devour a large frog she found at the edge of the stream, and to crunch it down, bones and all, in a couple of mouthfuls. Then she drank the cold, clear water of the mountain stream, lapping at it thirstily.

When she came to the little temple, the monk was chopping firewood for his brazier.

Remaining a safe distance from the monk, for his axe-blade was sharp, she said, clearly, as people talk, "May you dream only propitious dreams in the days to come, dreams of good omen and great fortune."

The monk smiled at the fox. "I am grateful for your wishes," he said. "Although it is not for me to know if my dreams shall be dreams of good fortune or otherwise."

The fox stared at him for some time with her green fox eyes. "I shall not be far," she said at length. "Should you need me."

And when the young monk looked up again from his firewood, she was gone.

Chapter three

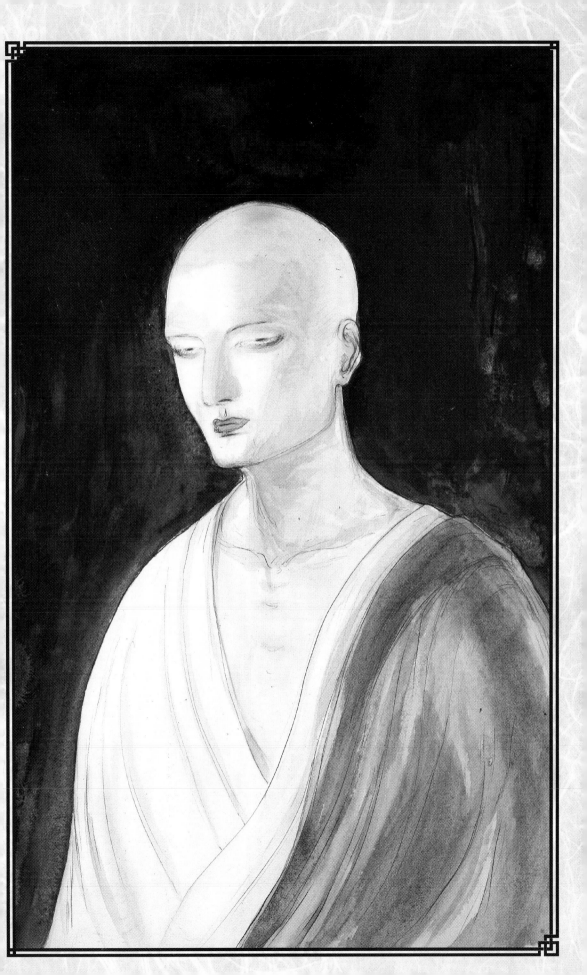

ar to the south and the west, in his house in Kyoto, the Master of Yin-Yang, the *onmyoji*, burned a lamp at a small table, upon which he had placed a square of painted silk, and upon it a lacquer chest and a black wooden key. Arranged according to the five cardinal points of the compass were five small porcelain plates, upon three of which were powdered matter, upon one of which was a bead of liquid, and upon the last plate there was nothing at all.

The onmyoji was a rich man. He was a high official in the Bureau of Divination, and many sought his advice and his favours. The governors of many provinces were grateful to him, and believed that his influence and his fortune-telling had given them their fortunes or their high positions. He had the ear of the Chancellor, and of the Ministers of the Right and the Left. But he was not a happy man.

He had a wife, who lived in the northern wing of his house, who ran his household judiciously and efficiently and who treated him in every way as a wife should treat a husband. He had a concubine, who was barely seventeen, and who was very beautiful: her skin was as pale as the palest plum-blossom, her lips were dark as plums. His wife and his concubine lived together, under the same roof, and they did not quarrel. But the onmyoji was not a happy man.

He lived in what was widely said to be the seventeenth-finest house in Kyoto. Spirits and demons of the air, *Oni* and *Tengu* alike, were ordered by him, and would obey his orders. He could remember every detail of two of his previous lives. As a young man he had travelled to China to study, and he had returned with his hair prematurely grey but with an unequaled knowledge of portents and omens. He was respected by those who were his superiors, and feared by those who were his inferiors. But, with all this, the onmyoji was not happy.

And this was because the onmyoji was afraid.

Ever since he could remember, since he was a tiny child, he had been afraid, and every thing he learned, every scrap of power he obtained, he had gathered in the hope that it would drive away the fear. But the fear remained. It waited behind him, and in the heart of him; it was there when he slept and there to greet him when he woke in the morning; it was there when he made love, and when he drank, and when he bathed.

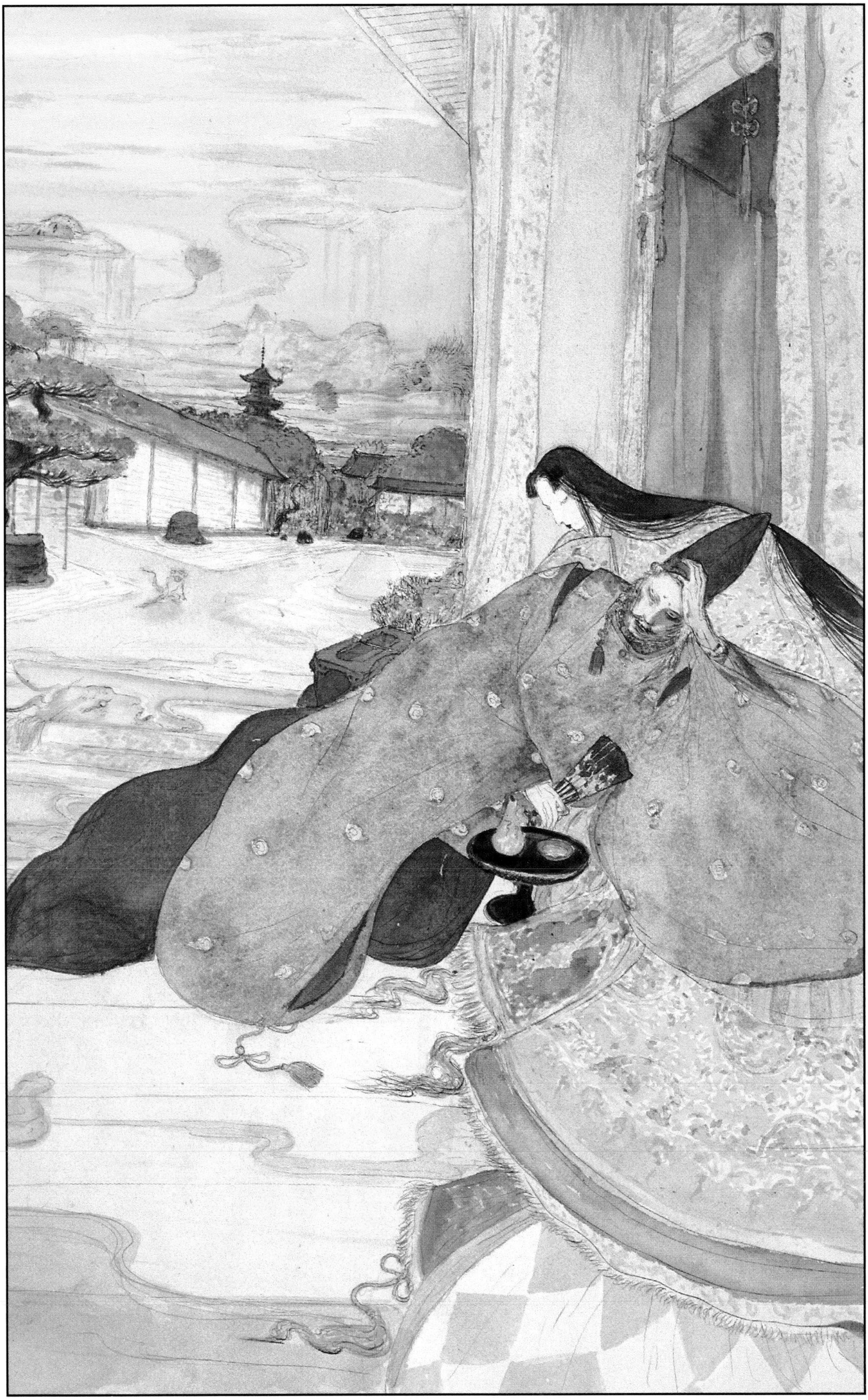

It was not a fear of death, for in his heart he suspected that death might be an escape from the fear. And there were days when he wondered if, by his arts, he were to kill every man, woman and child in the world, that the fear would be gone, but he suspected that the fear would still haunt him even if he were alone.

It was fear that drove him, and fear that pushed him into the darkness.

The Master of Yin-Yang sought knowledge from the defilers of graves. He met with misshapen creatures in the twilight, and he danced their dances, and he partook of their feasts.

On the outskirts of the city, where thieves and brigands and the unclean lived, the Master of Yin-Yang kept a dilapidated house, and in that house there were three women: one old, one young, and one who was neither young nor old. The women sold herbs and remedies to women who found themselves in unfortunate situations. It was whispered that unwary travellers who stopped in that house for the night were often never seen again. Be that as it may, no man knew of the onmyoji's involvement with the three women, nor of his visits to the house on those nights when the moon was dark.

In his head, and in his heart, the onmyoji was not an evil man. He was frightened. And the fear stole the joy from any moments of pride or happiness, and leeched the pleasure from his life.

One night, several weeks before the events previously related, when the moon was at its darkest, he had asked the three women in the dilapidated house the questions that troubled him most.

The wind blew through the broken screens, and howled in the rotting eaves.

"How can I find peace?" he asked the oldest of the women.

"There is peace in the grave," she told him, "and a momentary peace in the contemplation of a fine sunset."

She was naked, and her breasts hung like empty bags upon her chest, and on her face she had painted the face of a demon.

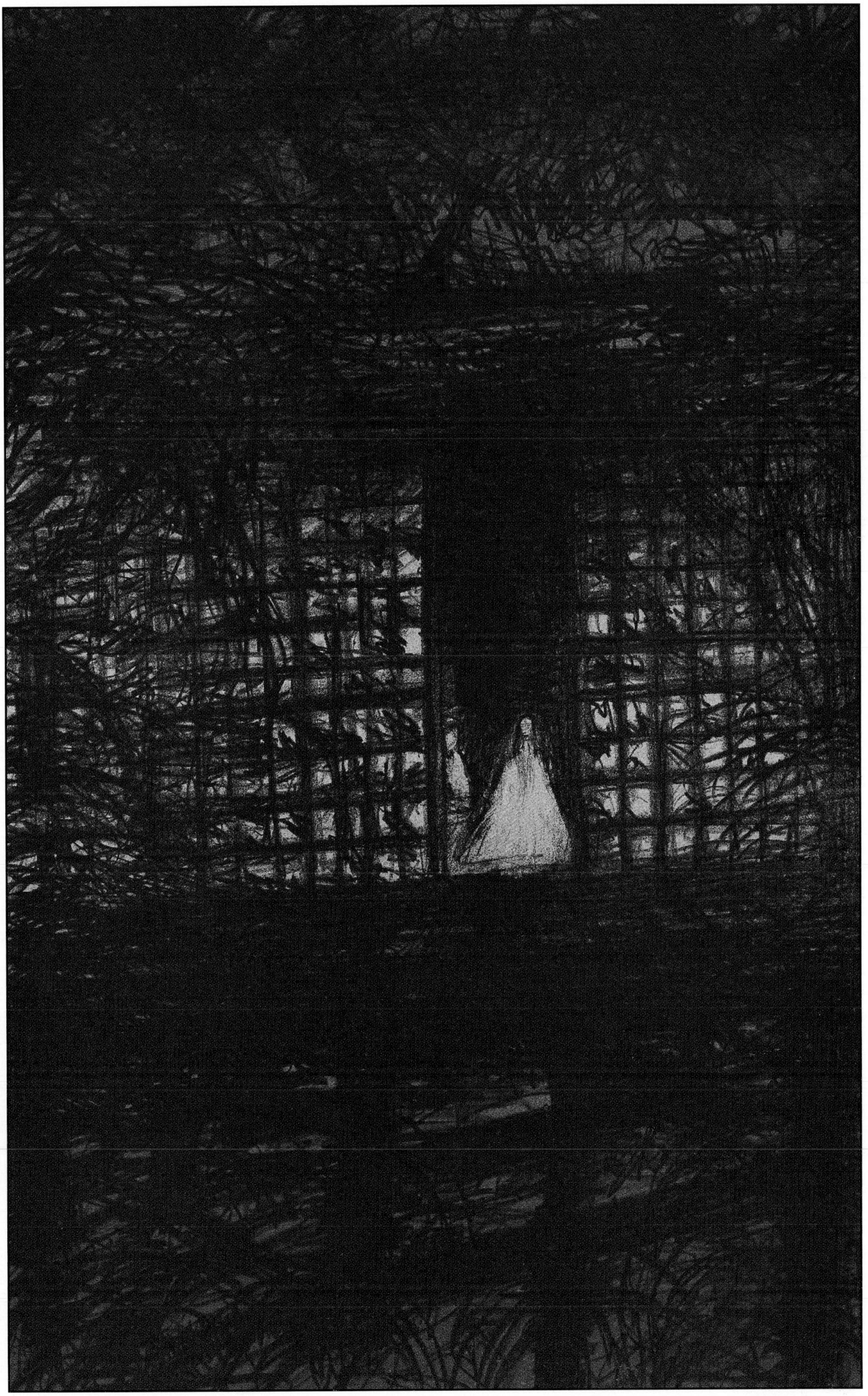

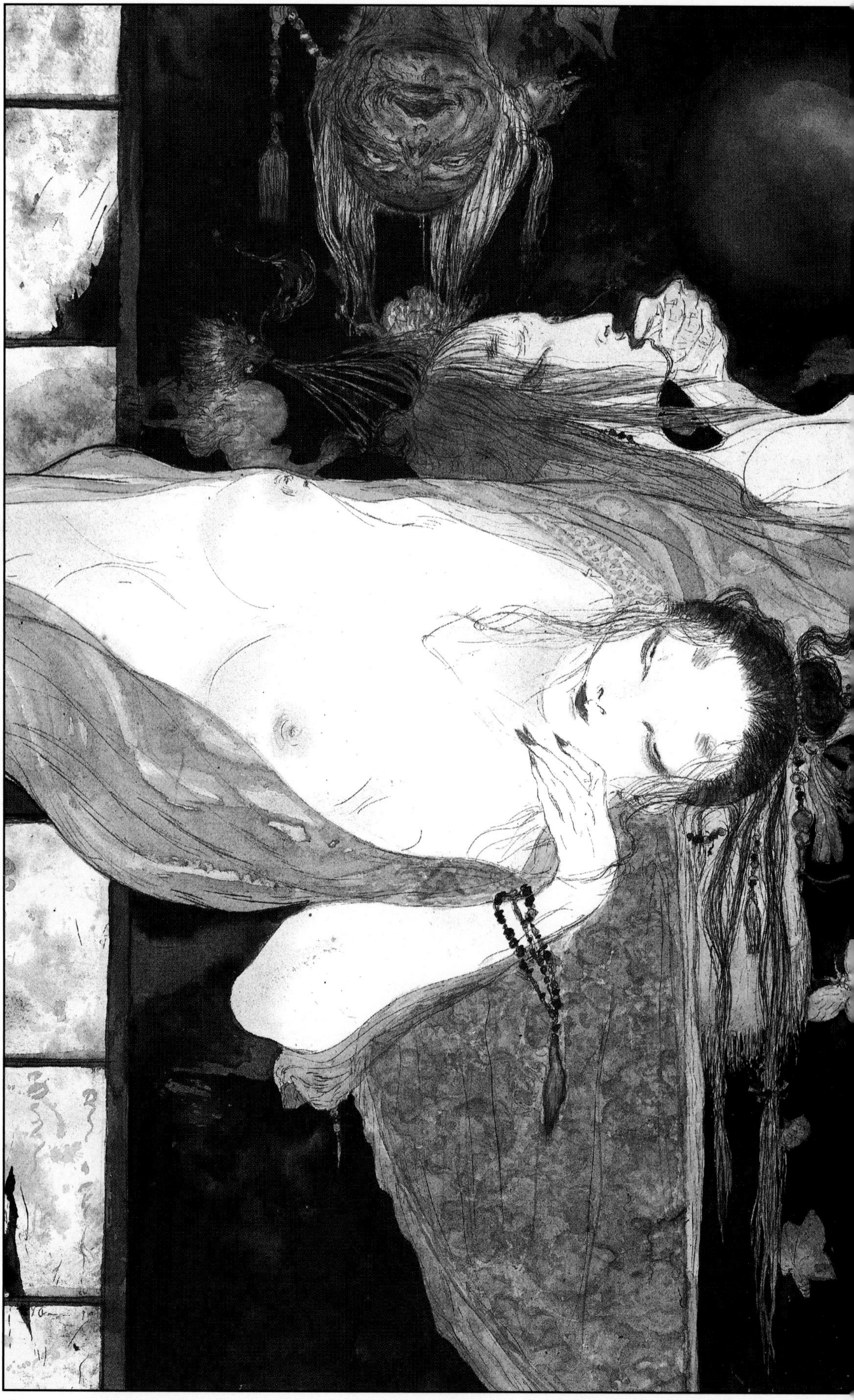

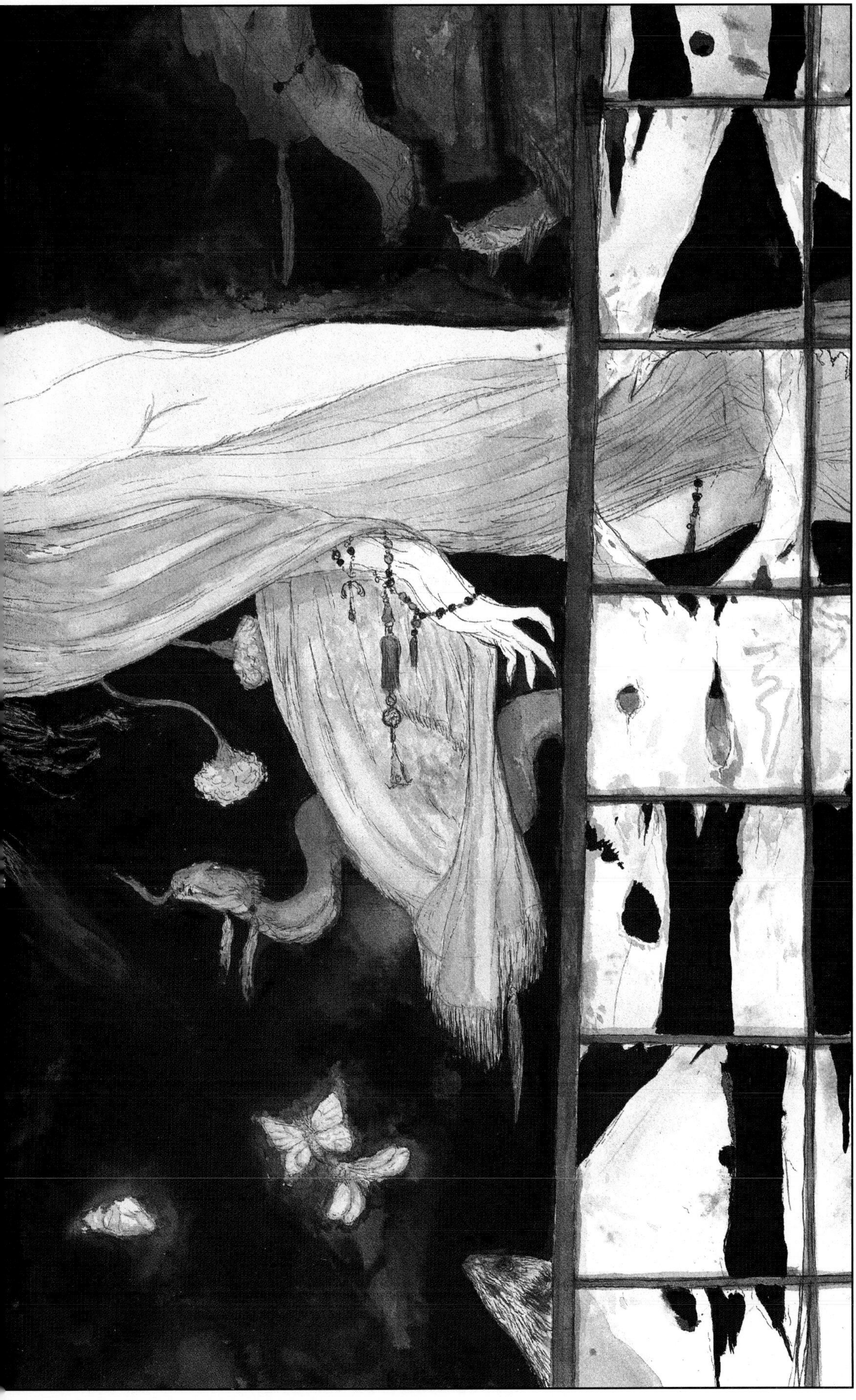

The onmyoji scowled, and tapped his fan into the palm of his hand impatiently.

"Why do I have no peace?" he asked the youngest of the three women.

"Because you are alive," she told him, with her cold lips. The onmyoji was most afraid of the youngest of the three women, for he suspected that she was not alive. She was beautiful, but it was a frozen beauty. If she touched him, with her cold fingers, he shuddered.

"Where can I find peace?" he demanded of the woman who was neither young nor old.

She was not naked, but her robe was open, and down her chest curved two rows of breasts, like the breasts of a she-pig or a rat, her many nipples black and hard as so many lumps of charcoal.

She sucked the air in through her teeth, and held it in, and then, after too long a time, she exhaled. And she said, "In the Province of Mino, many, many long days of travel away from here, to the north and the east, on the side of such and such a mountain is a small temple. It is of so little importance that it has but one monk tending to it. He is afraid of nothing, and he has the peace you desire. Now, I can weave it so that when he dies you will gain his strength, and you will fear nothing. But once I have woven, you will have only until the next full of the moon to cause his death. And he must die without violence, and without pain, or the weaving will fail."

The onmyoji grunted, satisfied. He fed her several small delicacies with his own hand, and stroked her hair, and told her that he was satisfied with this.

The three women withdrew into another part of the tumbledown house, and when they returned again it was almost dawn, and the sky was beginning to lighten.

They handed the onmyoji a square of woven silk, pale as moonlight. On it was painted the onmyoji and the moon, and the young monk.

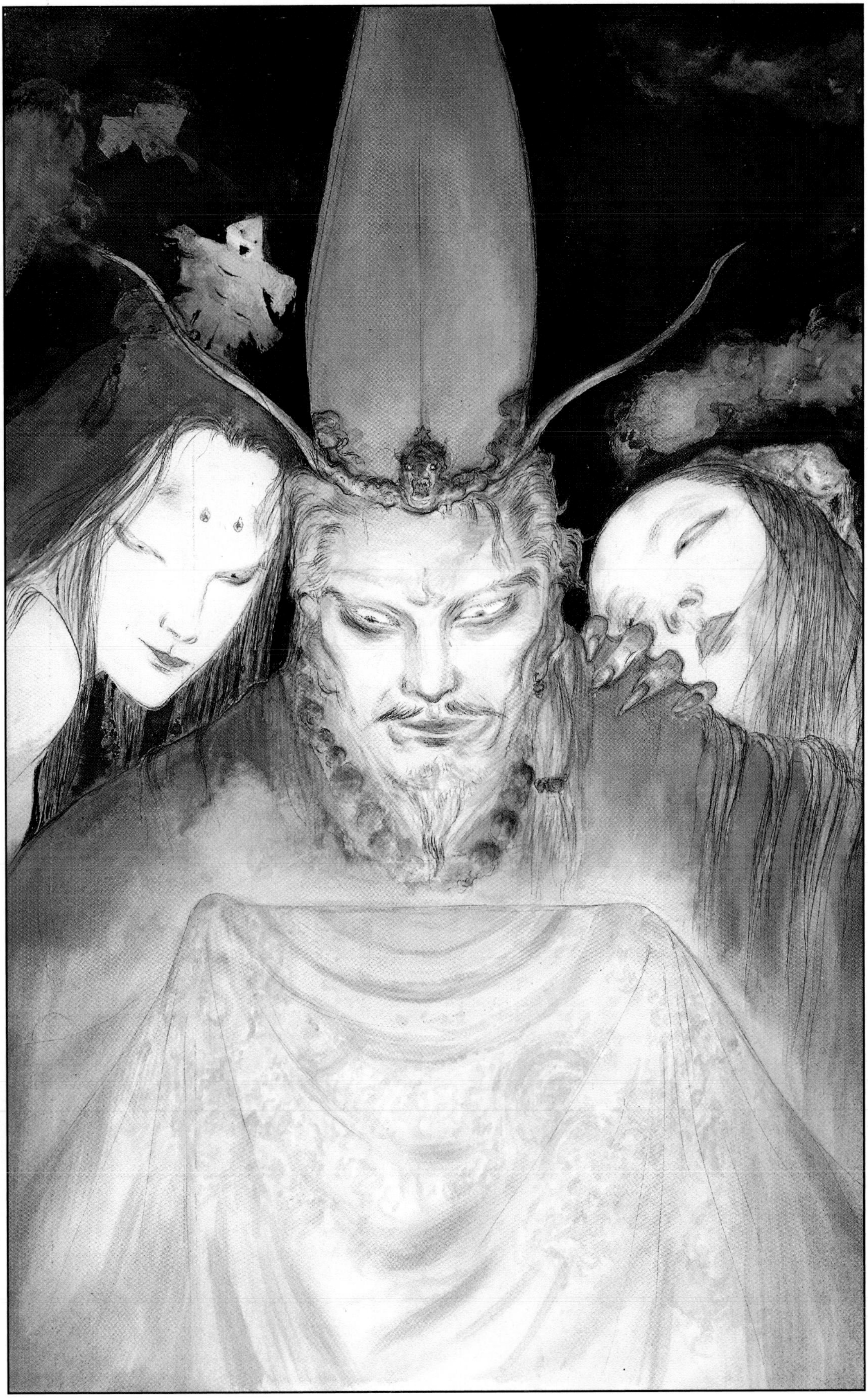

The onmyoji nodded, satisfied. He would have thanked them, but he knew that one must not thank creatures of their kind, so he placed their payment on the floor of their house, and hurried home, to be there before daybreak.

Now, there are many ways to kill at a distance, but most of them, even if they do not involve direct violence, involve the infliction of pain.

The Master of Yin-Yang consulted his scrolls. Then he sent his demons to the mountain where the monk lived, to obtain for him things that the monk had touched. (That was where the fox had overheard them.) And here, and now, the onmyoji sat in front of the little table, with the lamp upon it, and the lacquer box, and the key. One by one, he added a pinch of the substance in the little porcelain plates to the fire of the lamp — a pinch for each of the five elements. And the final pinch was from the last thing the demons had stolen from the monk: it was from the plate with nothing in it, which contained a scrap of the monk's shadow, that the demons had stolen from him.

With each pinch of powder the onmyoji added to the flame, it burned higher and brighter; and when he added the final pinch of nothing, which was the monk's shadow, the flame burned so high it filled the onmyoji's chamber with light, and then it was gone, leaving the room in darkness.

The onmyoji kindled a light and was pleased to observe that on the silk square that covered the table there was an unpleasant stain, as if something dead had been lying there over the face of the young monk.

He observed this with satisfaction. Then he went to his bed and slept the night peacefully, and without fear. He was, for that night, content.

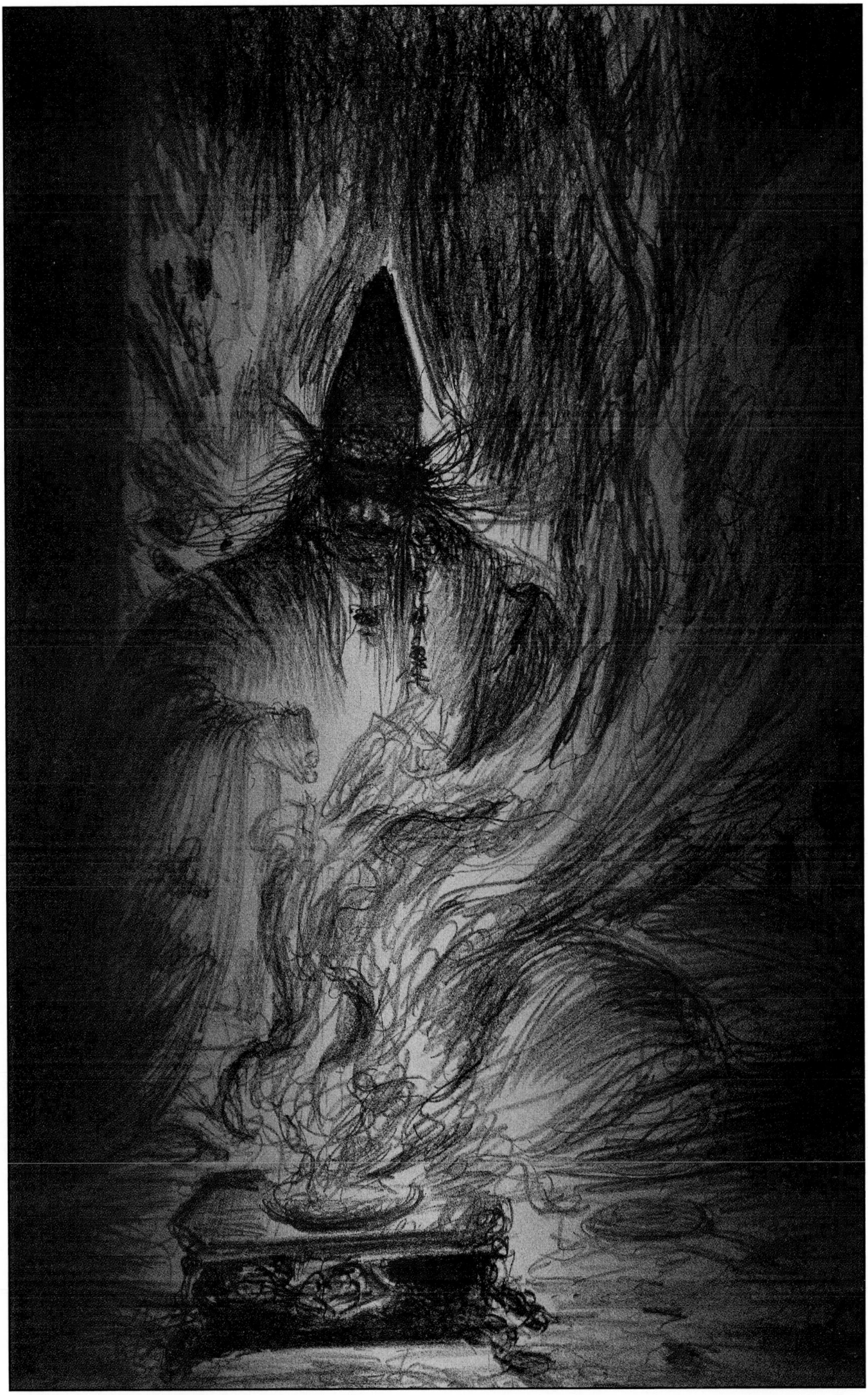

In the monk's dream that night, he was standing in his father's house, before his father had lost his house and all he owned in his disgrace, for his father had had powerful enemies.

His father bowed to him, and the monk remembered, in his dream, that his father had died by his own hand, and he also remembered that he, the monk, was still alive. He tried to tell his father this, but his father indicated, without words, that he could not listen to anything his son could tell him.

Then he produced from inside his robe a small lacquer box, and he held it out for his son to take.

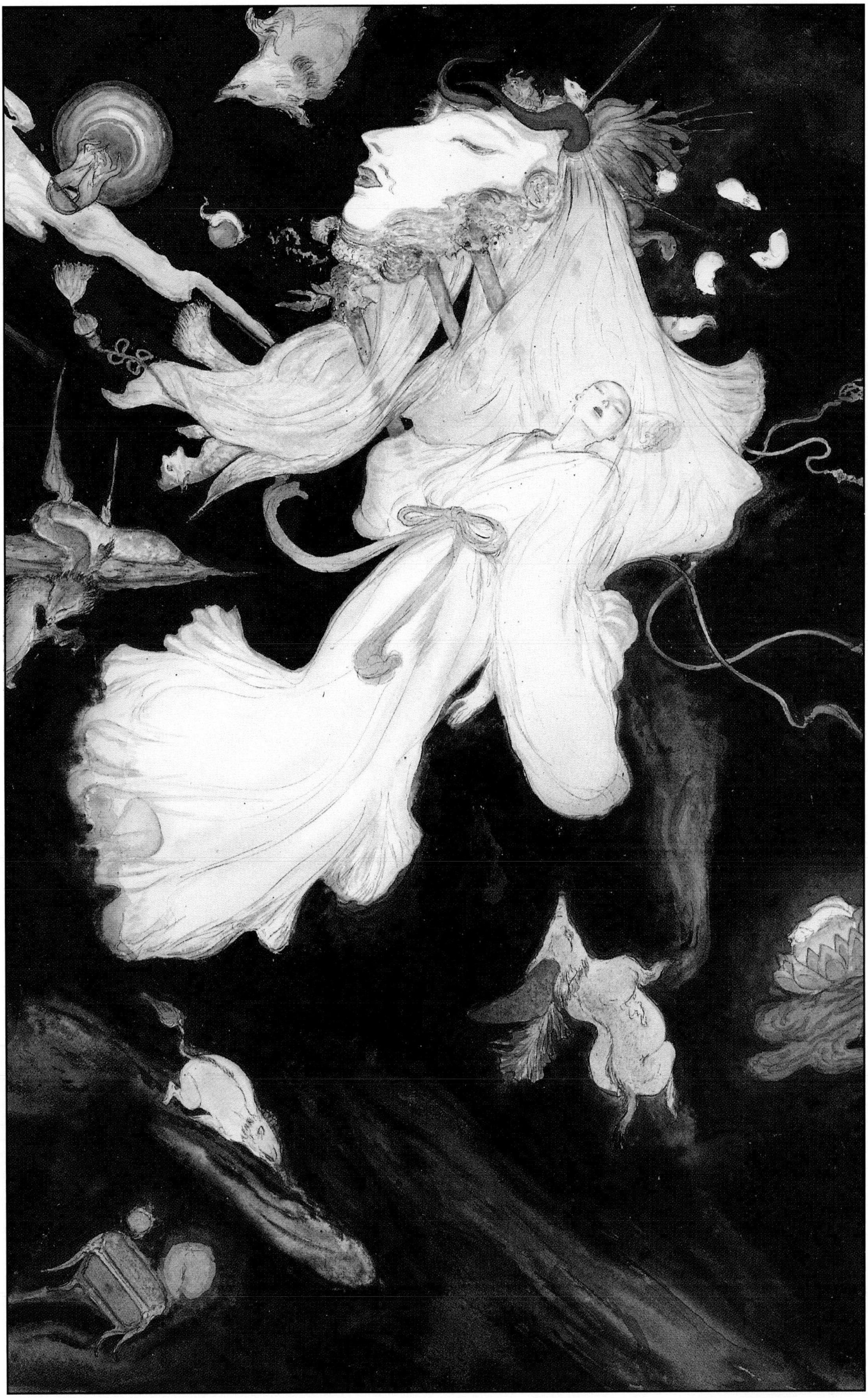

The monk took the enamel box, and his father was no longer there, but he gave no thought to this, for the enamel box took all his thoughts (although, in his dream, he thought he saw the flick of a fox's tail through an open door).

He knew there was something important inside the box. There was something he needed to see. But the box resisted all his efforts to open it, and the more he tugged and pried the more frustrated he was.

When he woke he felt troubled and discomfited, wondering if the dream was an omen or a warning. "If it was an evil dream," said the monk, "then may a Baku take it."

Then he rose, and went out to bring in water, and began his day.

On the second night the monk dreamed that his grandfather had come to him, although his grandfather had died, choking on a *mochi*, a small rice cake, when the monk was little more than a baby.

They were standing on a tiny island that was little more than a black rock in the sea. His grandfather stared out to sea with blind eyes. The sea birds wailed and cawed over the howl of the sea-wind and the splash of the spray.

His grandfather opened one old hand, to reveal a small black key. Slow as a mechanical toy he put his hand forward. The monk took the key from his grandfather. A seagull screeched three sad descending notes, and the monk would have asked his grandfather what they signified, but the old man had gone.

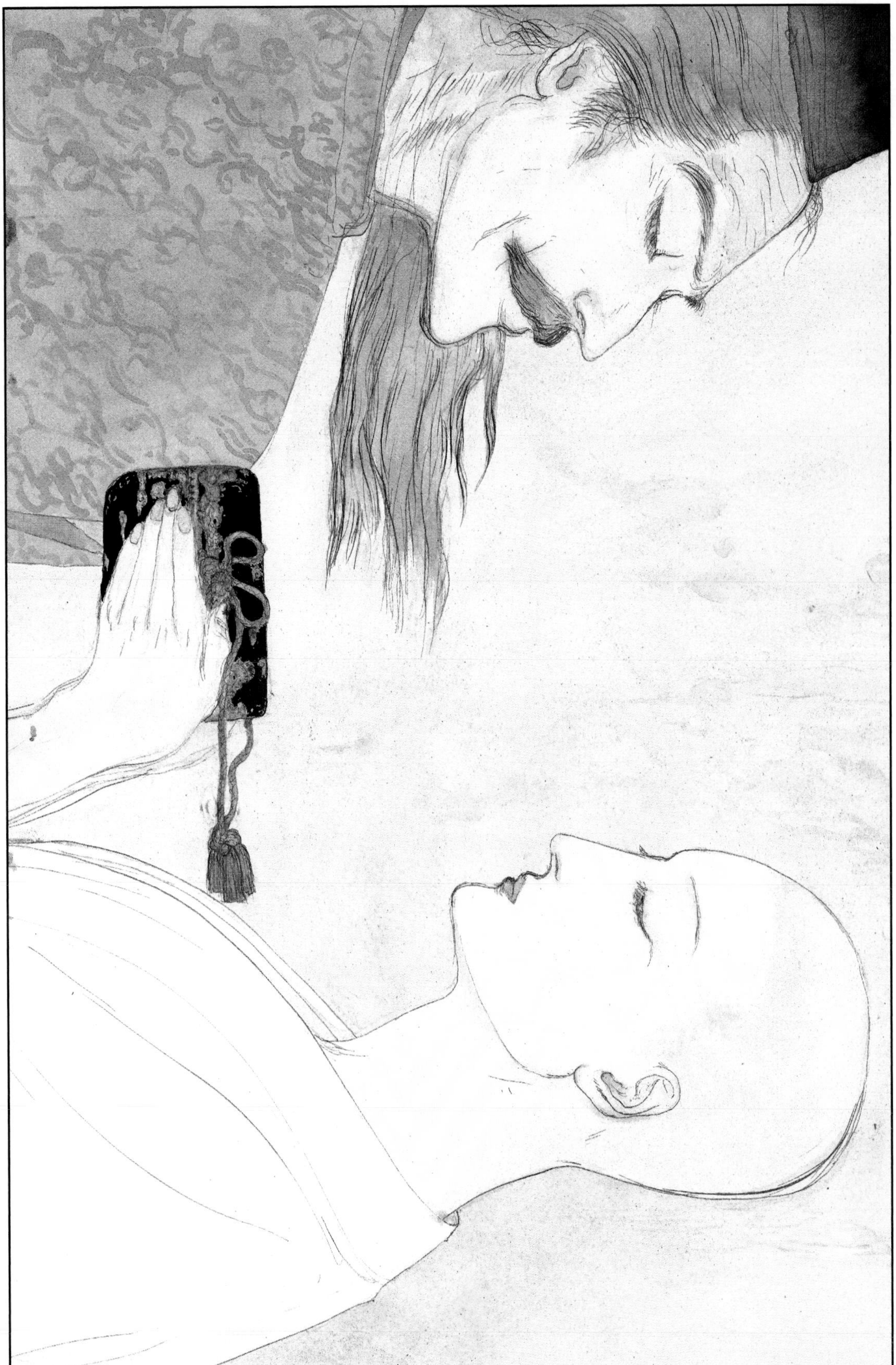

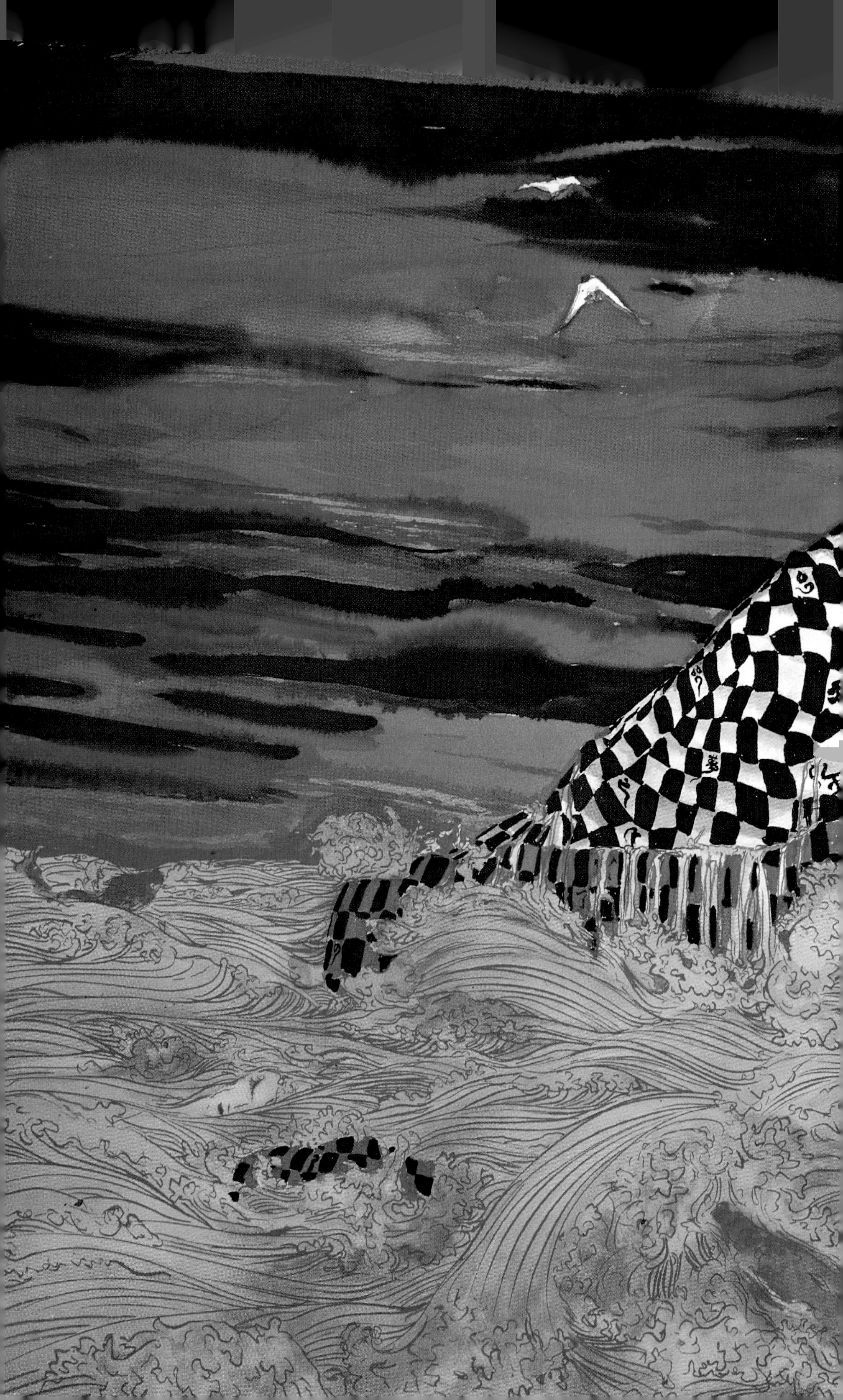

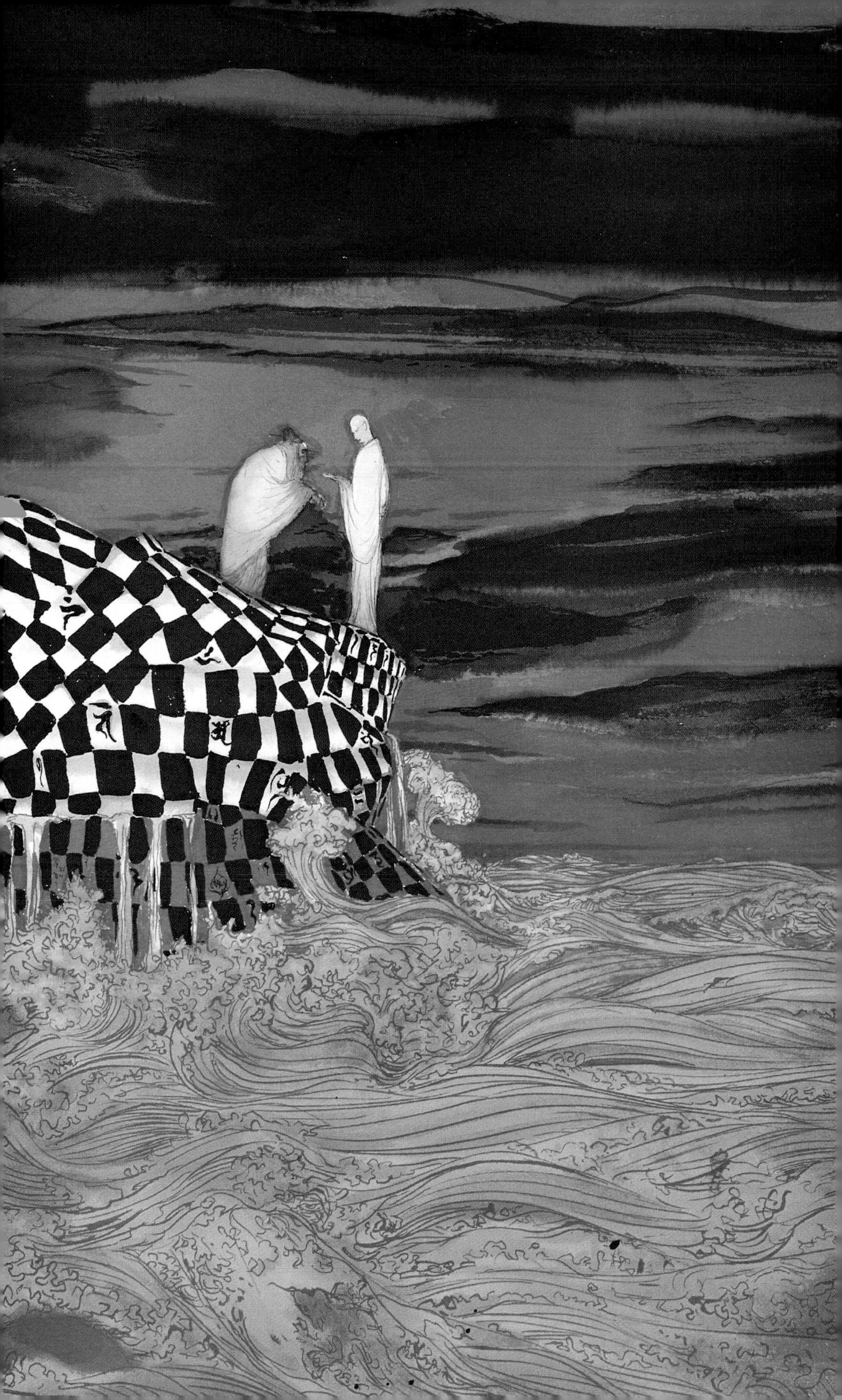

The monk held the key tightly. He looked about for something that the key would fit, but the island was barren and empty. The monk walked about the island slowly, seeing nothing.

And then it came to the monk that he was being watched, in his dream, and he looked around him, but there was nothing in his dream, save for the distant seagulls and a tiny figure on a distant cliff which might, the monk thought, have been a fox.

He woke with his hand closed about a nonexistent key, still feeling that the eyes of a fox were upon him.

The dream was so real that, later in the day, as a cold wind tumbled the first red and orange leaves from a maple tree into the temple's tiny vegetable garden, where the monk was tending the white and yellow gourds that grew in profusion, he found himself looking about him for the key, and only slowly realising that he had never touched or seen it in the waking world.

That night the monk expected another dark dream. As he closed his eyes he heard something at his door. And then he slept.

But for the first part of the night, he dreamed of nothing at all. And in the second part of the night he dreamed he was standing upon a bridge watching carp swimming placidly about a fishpond, and one of the carp was purest silver, and the other carp was purest gold, and it made the monk happy to watch them.

He woke, certain that the dream was a good omen, and relieved that the days of dark dreams were done with, and he smiled and was happy as he climbed from his sleeping mat.

The monk's good mood remained until he stumbled over the body of the fox, her eyes closed, stretched out across the threshold of the temple.

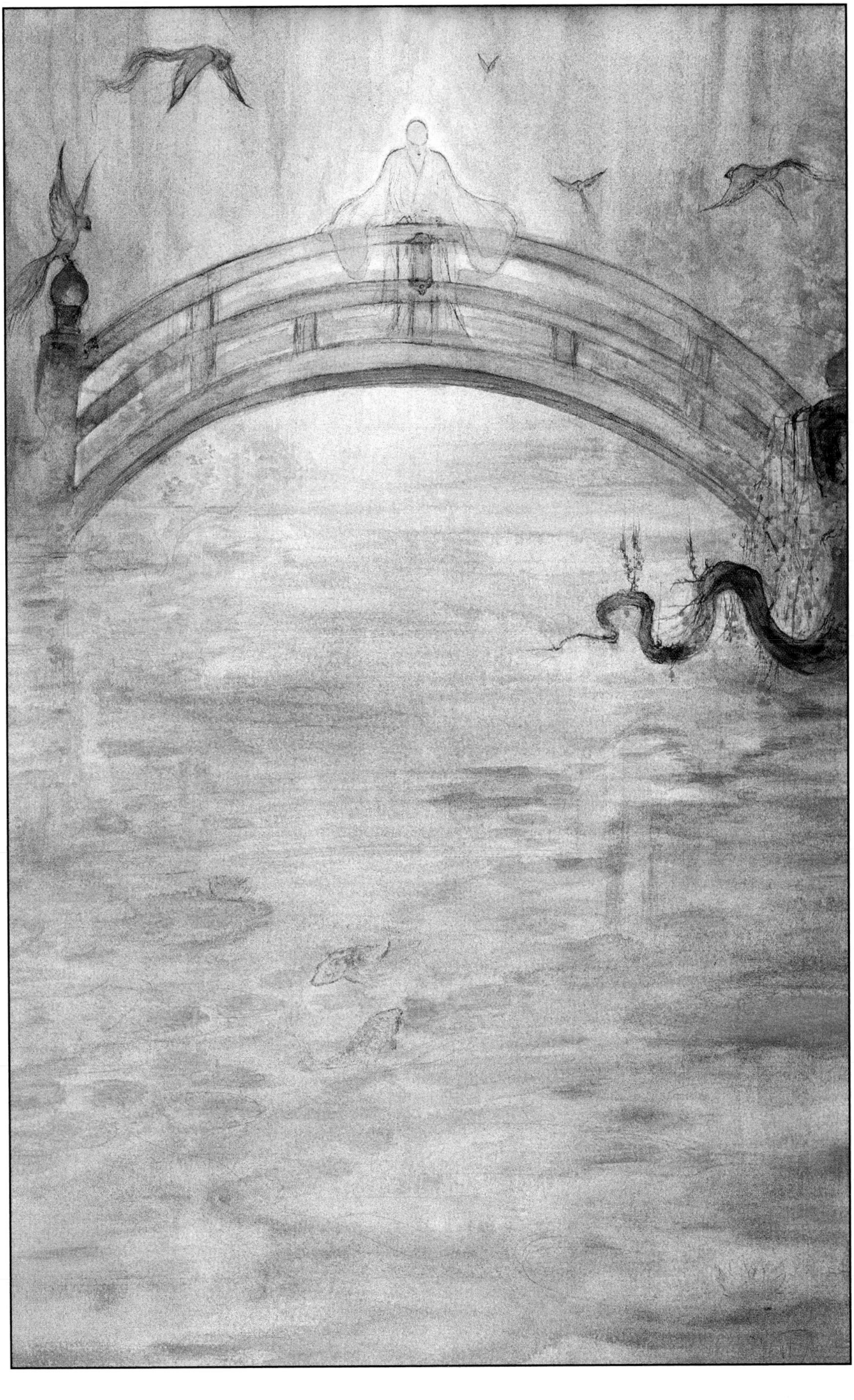

Chapter four

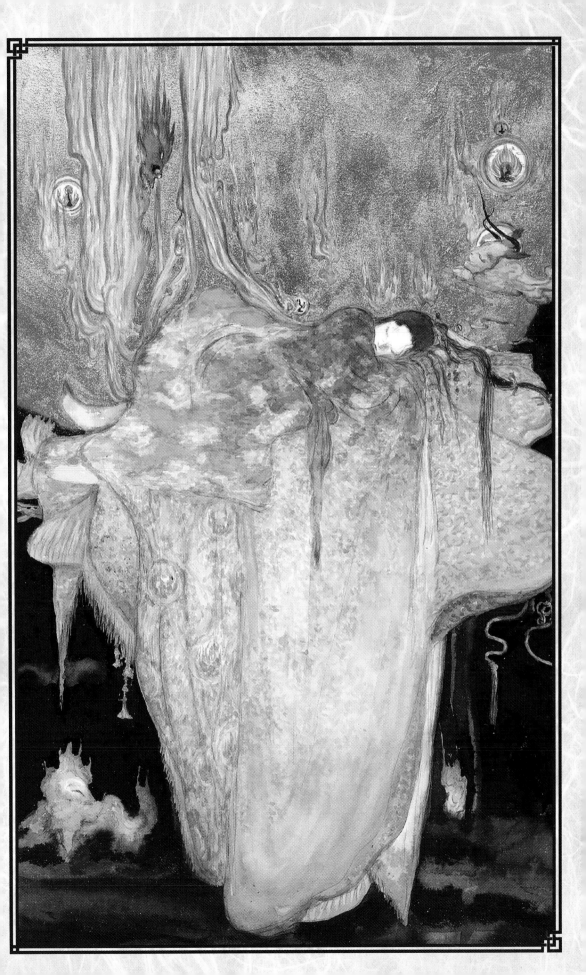

At first, the monk believed the fox was dead. Then, as he squatted beside her, he perceived that she was breathing, so shallowly and slowly that one could scarcely tell that she was breathing at all, but still, she was alive.

The monk took the fox into the little temple, and set her down beside the brazier, to warm herself. Then the monk said a silent prayer to the Buddha, for the life of the fox, "For she was a wild thing," thought the monk, "but she had a good heart, and I would not see her die."

He stroked her fur, as soft as thistledown, and felt the weak beat of her heart.

"When I was a boy," said the monk to the unconscious fox, "before my father's disgrace, I would, from time to time, run away from my nurse and from my teachers, and I would go to the market, where they sold live animals: in bamboo cages I saw all manner of beasts — foxes and dogs and bears, small monkeys and pink-faced monkeys, hares and crocodiles, snakes and pigs and deer, herons and cranes and bearcubs. When I saw them it made me happy, for I loved the animals, but it also made me sad, for it hurt me to see them imprisoned like that.

"One day, after the merchants had packed their wares and gone for the day, I found a broken cage, and in it, a baby monkey, too scrawny even to have been sold for the pot, for it was dead — or so somebody must have thought. But I perceived that it lived, and so I concealed it in my breast and made my way to my father's house.

"I kept the monkey in my room, and I fed it scraps I saved from my own meals. He grew, my little monkey, until he seemed almost as big as I was. He was my friend. He would sit in the persimmon tree outside our house waiting for me to return. My father tolerated the monkey, and all went well until the day a certain lord came to the house to see my father.

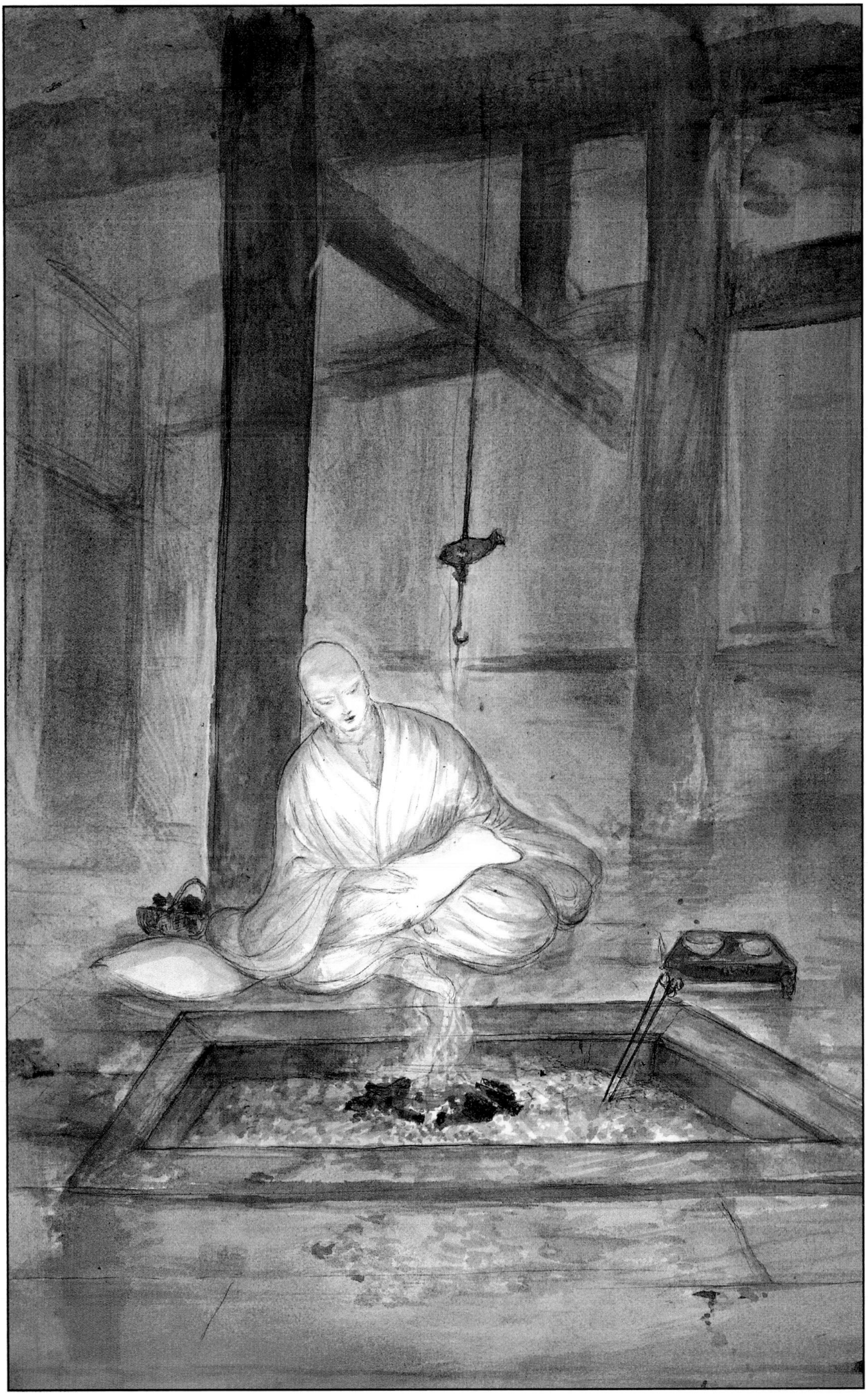

"The monkey seemed to go mad. He refused to let the lord approach my father. Instead he swung down and barred his way, baring his teeth and showing his chest, acting as if the lord were a rival from another tribe of monkeys.

"The lord gestured to one of his retainers, who pulled out his bow and put an arrow through the monkey's chest, although I begged him not to. I carried the monkey out of the house, and he looked into my eyes as he died.

"Later, when my father was disgraced, it was through the machinations of that selfsame lord. And sometimes I think that the monkey was not a monkey, but a spirit sent by Amida Buddha to protect us, and protect us it would have done if only we had listened and seen. This was long ago, little fox, before I was a monk, in a life that is dead to me, but still, we learn.

"And perhaps, with all your fox tricks, perhaps you also wished to protect me."

And then the monk said a prayer to Amida Buddha; and another prayer to Kishibojin, who was a demon before she encountered the Buddha, and who guards children and women; and to Dainichi-Nyorai; and, lastly, he said a brief prayer to Binzuru Harada, who was the first of the Buddha's disciples, whom the Buddha had forbidden to enter Nirvana. He said his prayers to all these entities, imploring their aid and their intercession for the little fox.

And at the end of all his praying, the fox still lay, limp and still on the matting, like a dead thing.

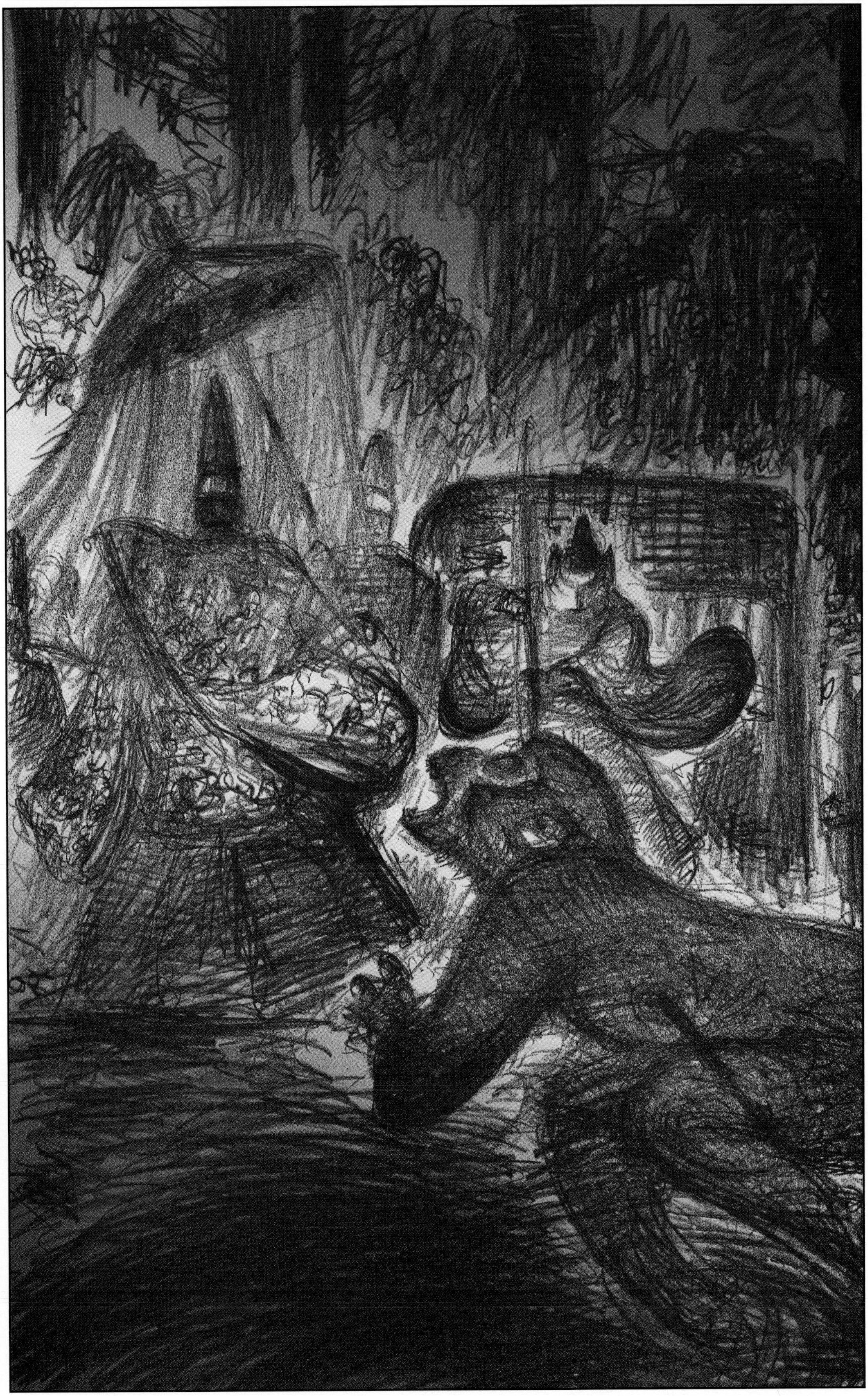

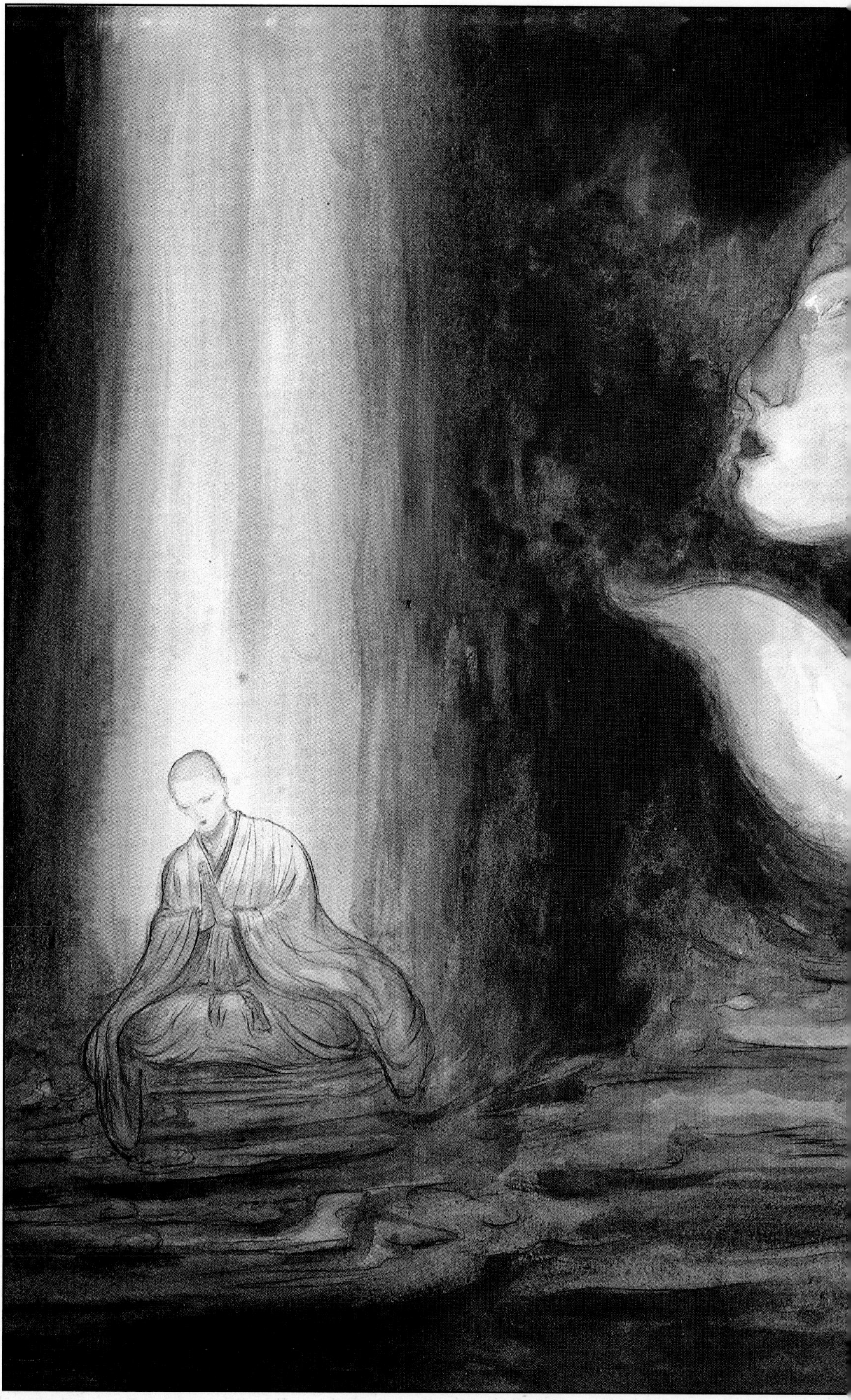

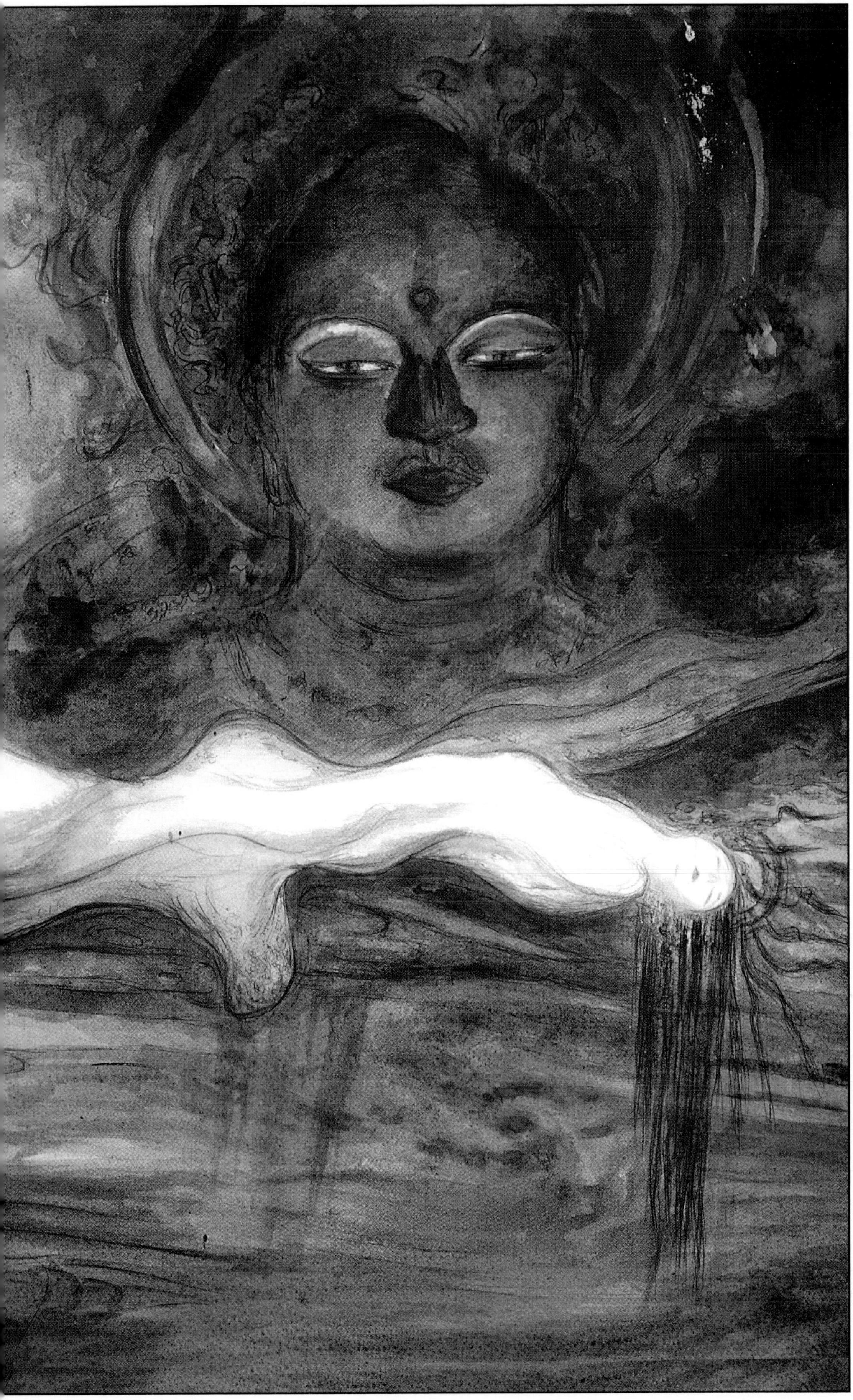

There was a village at the foot of the mountain, almost half a day's travel away. "Perhaps," thought the monk, "there will be a doctor or a wise woman in the village, who can help the fox." And without a second thought he picked up the limp fox and began to carry her down the mountain track that would eventually take him to the village.

It was chilly, and the monk shivered in his thin robes. Large flies, the last and oldest and most unpleasant flies of the year, buzzed about him, following him down the track, doing their best to annoy him.

Half the way down the mountain the mountain stream became a small river, and there was a bridge over this river. As the monk approached the bridge he saw an old man coming up the track toward him. The old man had a long white beard, and long, long eyebrows, and he leaned on a tall, carved stick as he walked. There was an air about him of wisdom and of serenity, but there was also an air of mischief, or so it seemed to the monk.

The old man waited on the bridge for the monk to reach him.

"The maple trees are very beautiful," said the old man. "So many colours, and so soon they will be gone. Sometimes I think that the autumn can be equally as beautiful as the spring."

The monk agreed that this might be so.

"Now, what is that that you are carrying?" asked the old man. "It looks like a dead dog. Is that not an unclean thing for a monk to be carrying?"

"It is a fox," said the monk, "and she is not dead."

"And do you go to kill her?" asked the old man, gruffly.

"I go to seek a cure for her," said the monk. The old man looked very stern, and he raised the stick he carried and with it he hit the monk — once across the side of the head and once across the shoulders.

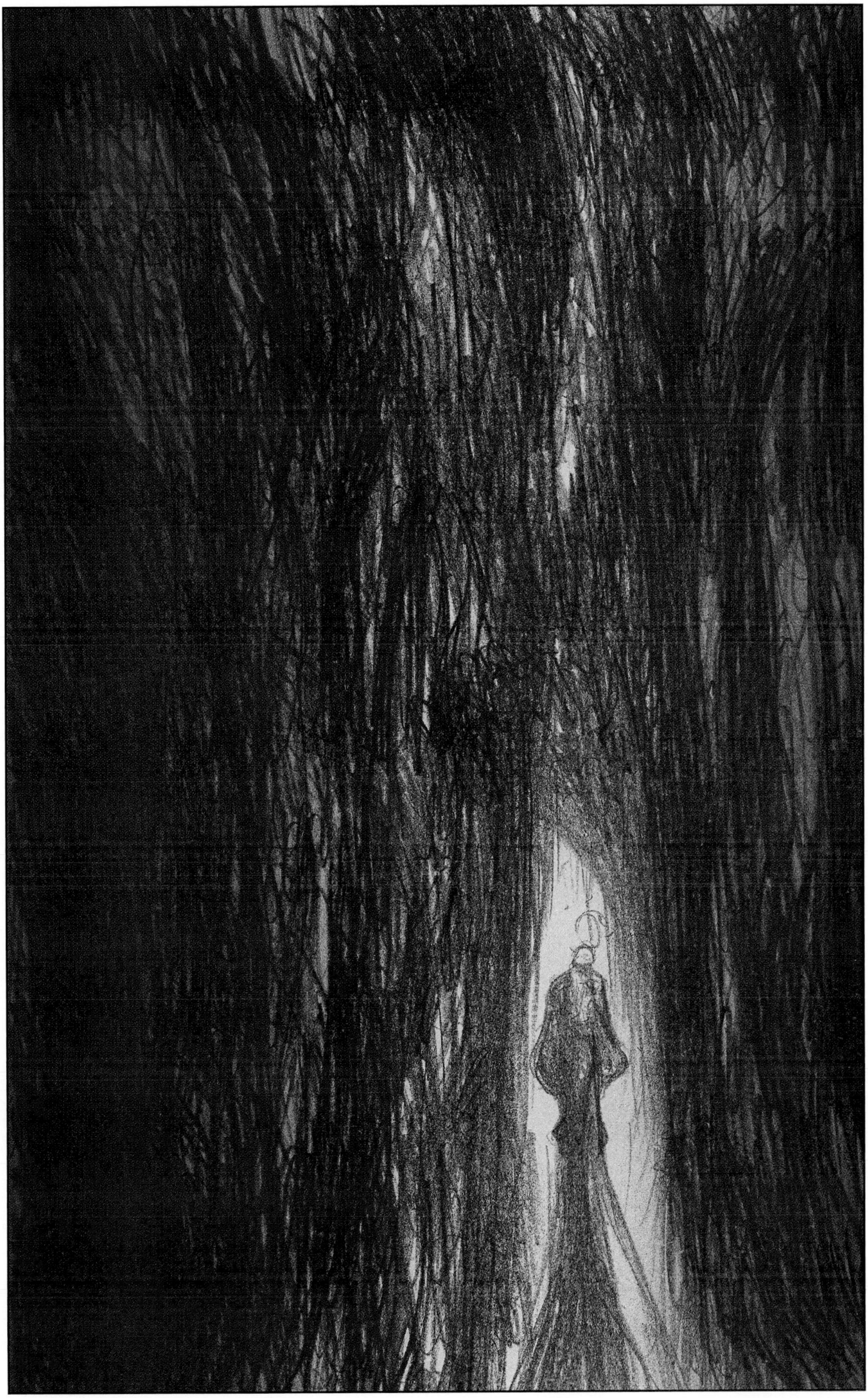

"*That!* is for deserting your temple," said the old man, with the first blow of the stick. "And *that!* is for meddling in the affairs of fox spirits."

The monk bowed his head. "You may be right to hit me," he said, "for it is as you say. I am not in my temple, and I am carrying a fox. But still, I believe I am doing the right thing, in trying to seek a cure for her."

"The right thing? The right thing?" And once again the old man hit the monk with the stick, this time prodding him in the chest with it. "Why, you ninny, you thoughtless creature. The right thing would be to return to your temple with the fox, and to sleep, with a token of the King of All Night's Dreaming beneath your head, for it is in dreams that your little fox-girl is trapped."

"If I can ask this, without receiving a commensurate blow to my person," said the monk, hesitantly, "where would I find a token of the King of All Night's Dreaming?"

The old man stared at the young monk, and then he looked at his carved stick, and then he sighed, long and loudly, like a very old man trying to cool hot soup. He reached into his sleeve and pulled out a strip of paper with something written upon it, and this paper he pressed into the monk's hand.

"There," grumbled the old man, "but you are still a fool, for the fox will die, or you will, and there is not a thing you can do on this earth or off of it that would change this, whether or not your motives are pure."

The monk was going to protest, to ask why the old man had given him the token if it could do no good, when he realised that he was alone on the bridge, and indeed, alone upon the mountainside.

"Then that old man must have been Binzuru Harada," thought the monk, for Binzuru Harada is often depicted as an old man with a white beard and long eyebrows; and he will do good on this Earth until one day the Buddha permits him to move on.

Still, the monk wondered why Binzuru Harada would have helped someone as insignificant as himself; and he took little comfort in recalling that it was for breaking his vow of chastity that Binzuru Harada was denied Nirvana.

The fox had weighed almost nothing on the journey down the mountainside, but as the monk turned to walk back up the mountain he found the body seemed to get heavier and heavier. A soft mist had descended upon the mountainside, blurring the edges of things. The monk placed one foot in front of the other, and he walked back up the mountain.

He wondered if he were doing the right thing, helping the fox. He did not know, but he knew that he could not abandon her. He had to try.

It was late in the afternoon by the time the monk reached the temple he had left early that morning. Autumn mists hung like cobwebs, or strands of raw silk, across the mountainside, and the encroaching twilight made the world feel doubly dreamlike.

Even the temple, in which the monk had spent the last eight years, seemed ghostlike as he entered it, as if it were somehow now an imaginary place. The brazier was almost cold: the monk added charcoal to it, and he cooked his rice over it, roasting some thinly-sliced gourd to accompany it.

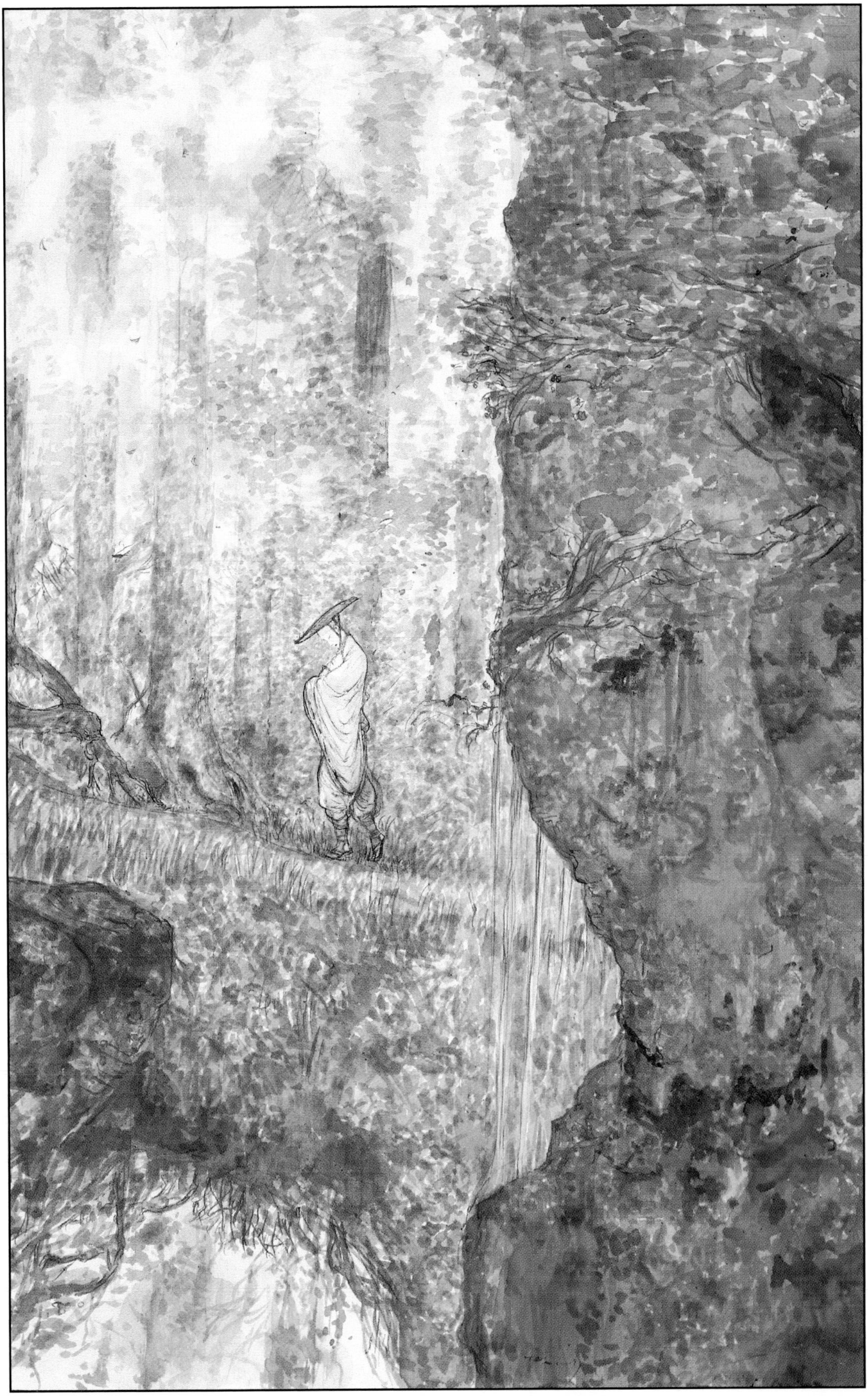

Then he made his evening devotions, although he made them with slightly less enthusiasm than usual. It is one thing to pray; it is another to pray to entities who might not only be listening, but who will search you out on the road and beat you across the head with sticks if you say something that offends them.

In the flickering light of the brazier, the monk experienced a strange illusion — it occurred to him that a scrap of his shadow was missing, gone as if it had been torn away.

The fox slept like a dead thing.

The fox was so small. He ran his hand across the softness of her fur. Then he inspected the strip of parchment that Binzuru Harada had given him. He could not read what was written there: the characters seemed to twist and shimmer as he looked at them, like characters in a dream.

The monk put the fox in his robe, so the heat of his body would keep her warm, and perhaps keep her alive. He lay down on his sleeping mat, and placed the slip of paper beneath his pillow, and, worn out from his walk first down the mountain and then up the mountain, he slept.

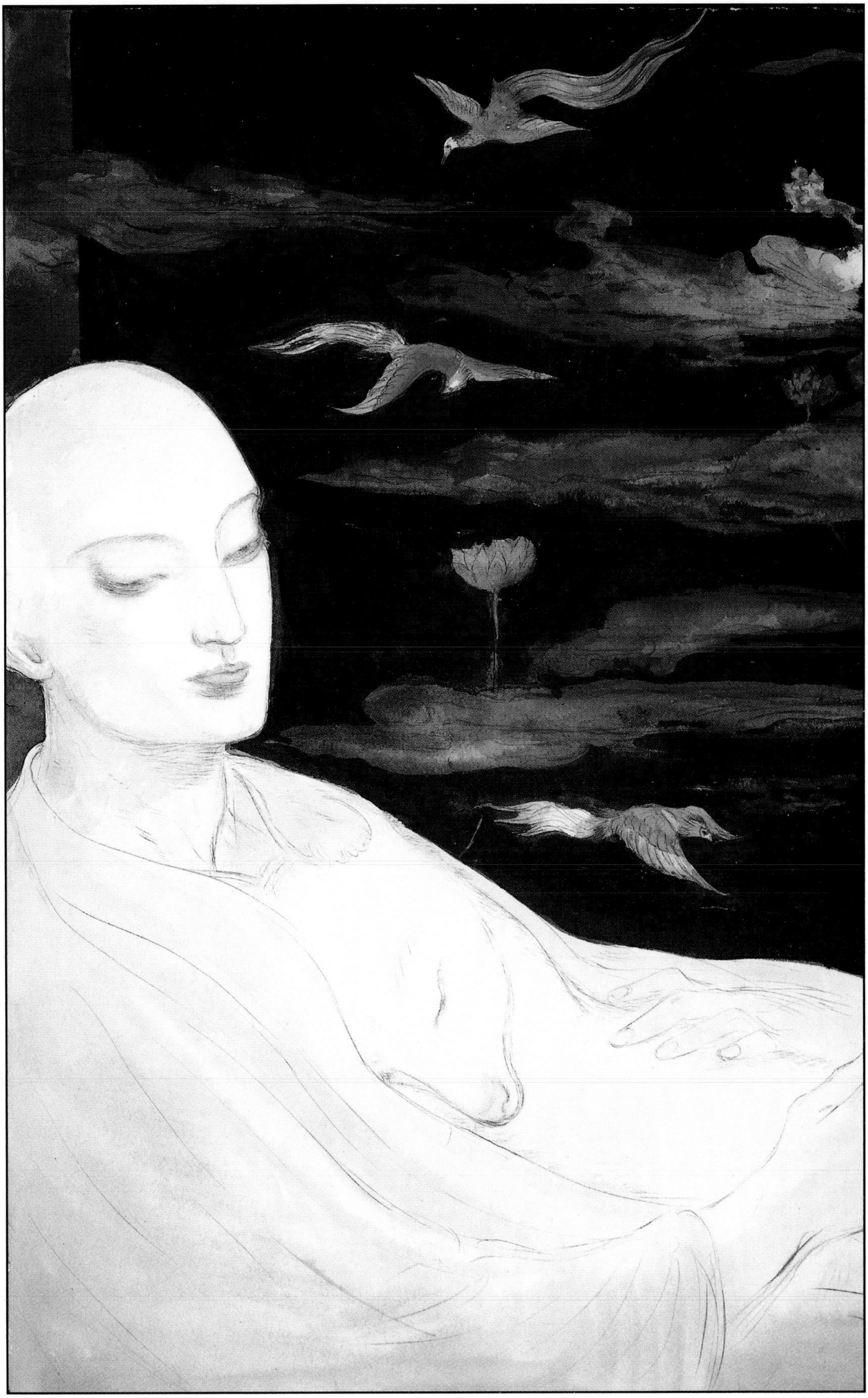

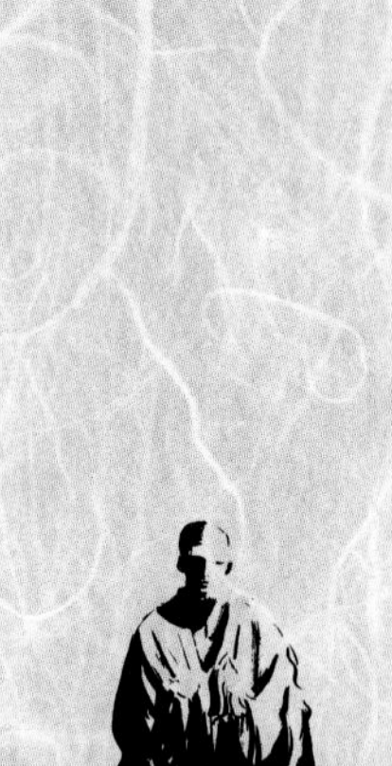

Chapter five

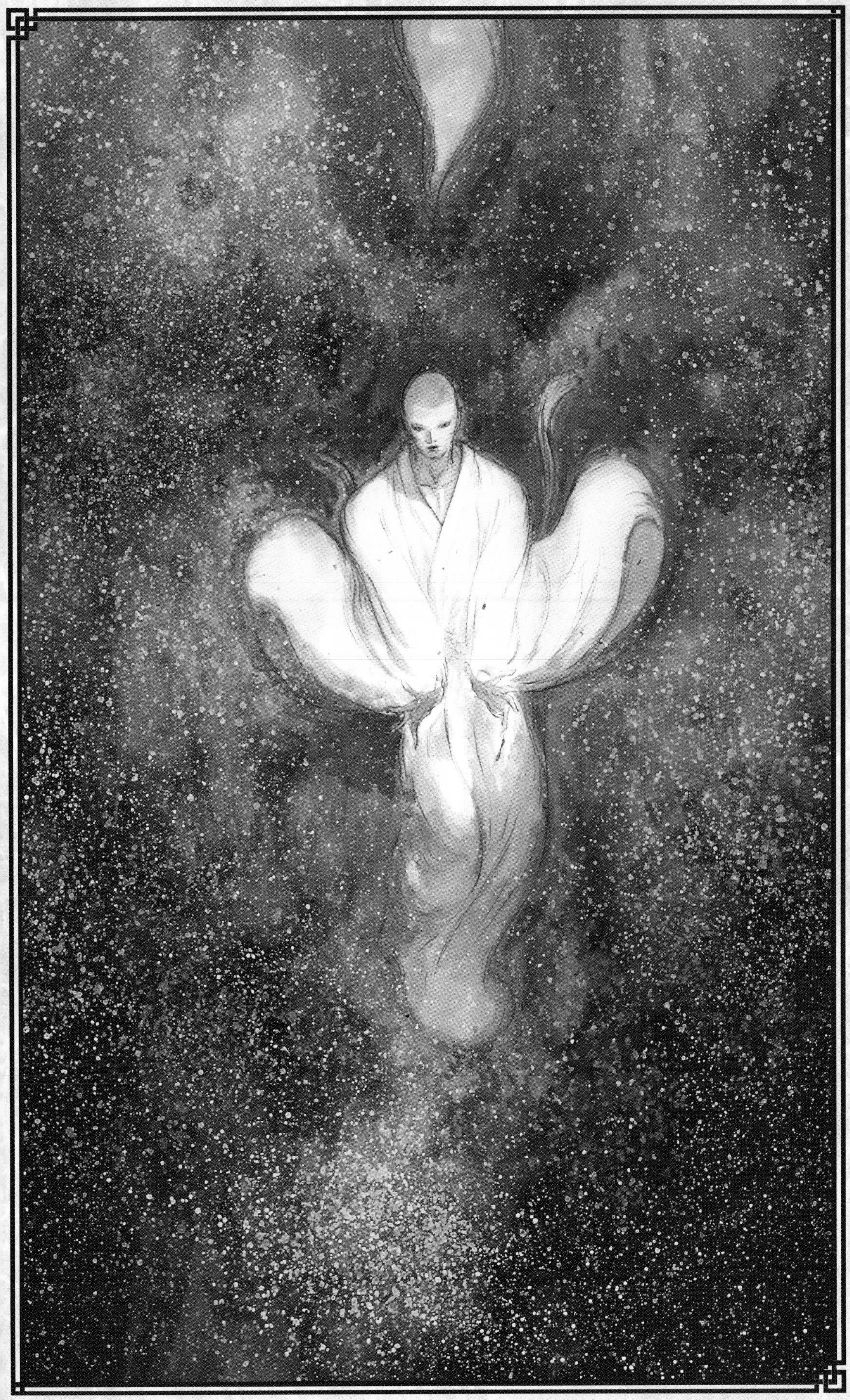

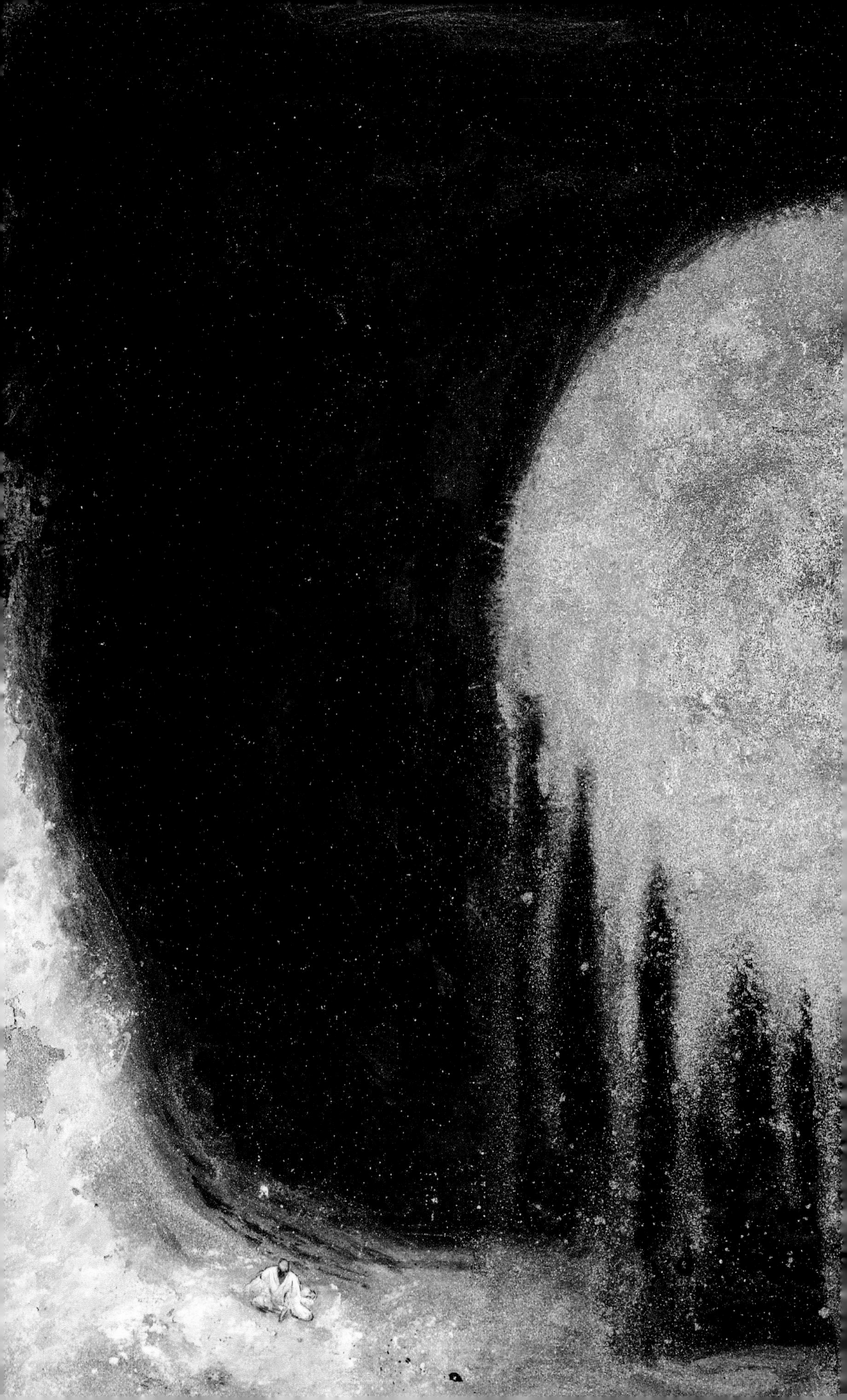

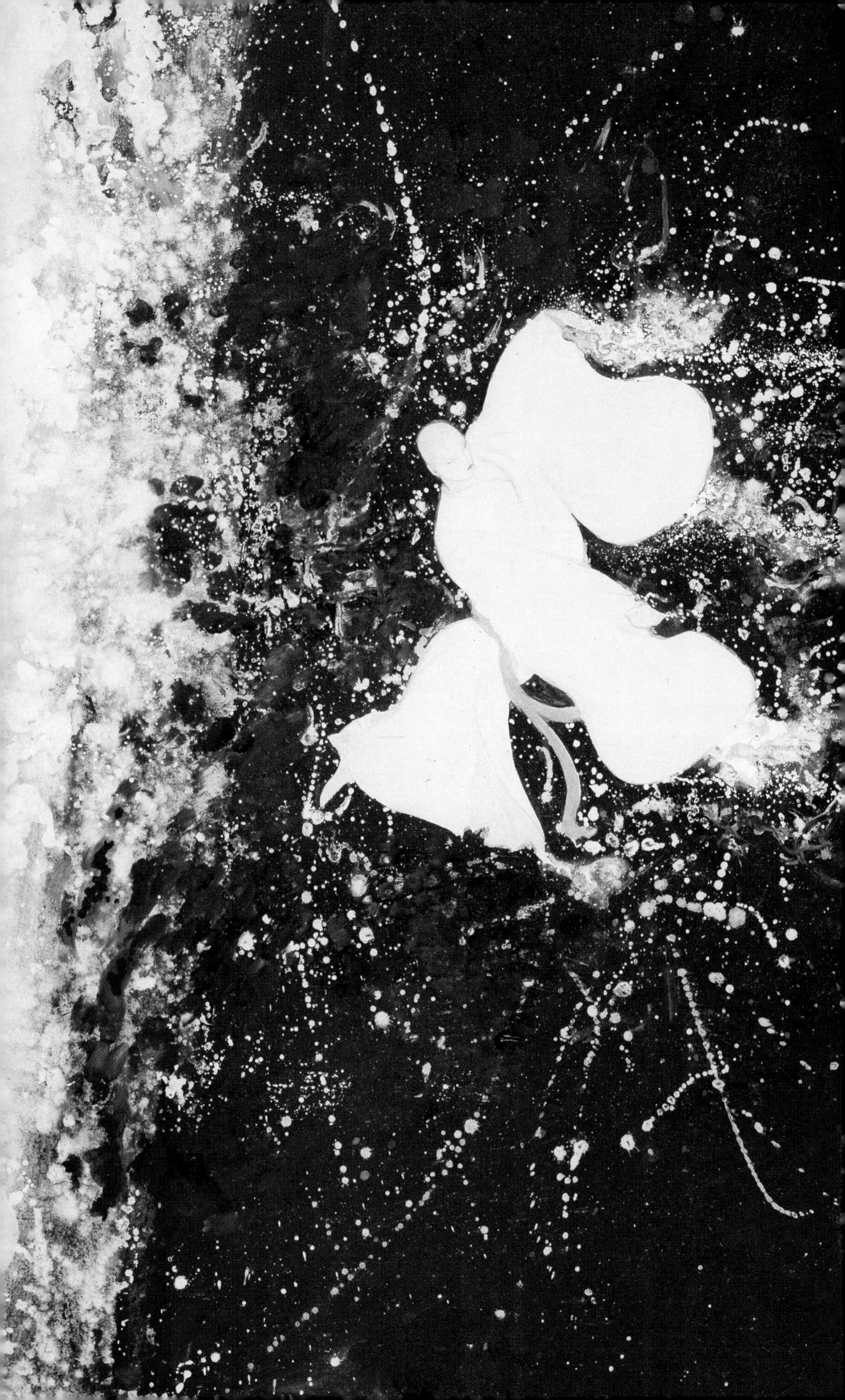

To begin, darkness.

In the darkness a light flickered into being. Then another, and another. The lights were moving.

They were fireflies. First a handful, then a swarm, and then hundreds and thousands of fireflies glittered with their cold fire in the darkness.

It reminded the monk of a river of stars, or a bridge of stars, or a ribbon, twining away into the darkness, insubstantial and glimmering, and it was along this ribbon that the monk began to walk.

In his hand he was holding a scrap of paper, which glowed even more brightly than the fireflies.

As he walked, the fireflies, which had been flickering on and off, began to fall away, to drop and to tumble like camellia blossoms.

The monk tumbled with them. He realised as he fell that he was not falling through fireflies, but through the Milky Way, the river of the gods that passes through the night sky.

He landed gently on a barren plain of rock, malachite-green.
He scrambled to his feet.

He began to walk across the glassy green plain. In his dream he was
wearing huge wooden sandals, of the kind that are worn in the rainy season,
to keep a person high up and out of the mud. As he walked the wooden
sandals were worn down and worn away, and soon he was walking
in his bare feet across the plain, which was sharp as a hundred knives,
and the blood ran from the soles of his feet, leaving red footprints behind him.

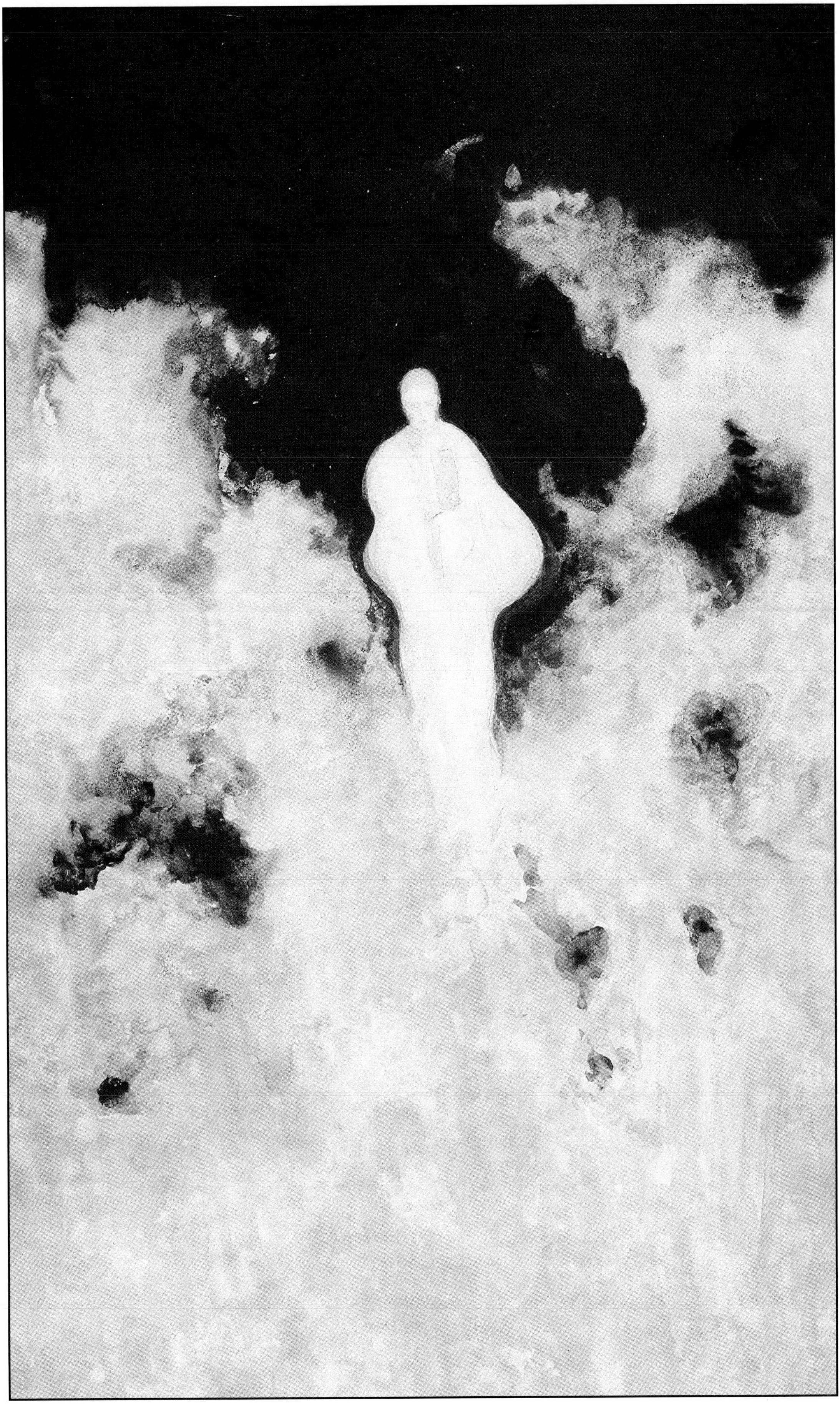

He walked thro[ugh] ...san or above our bones, jagged and shattered
and inhuman.

He walked thro[ugh] ...san... hot and sweet, and the air was
filled with biting ...ild...der than they could easily see,
which settled o[n] ...at the corners of his eyes and biting him,
raising welts wh... ...rom else... Soon the air was thick with the creatures.

His strip of pap[er] ...lightly as he held it high in front of him,
and he kept walk[ing]

And then he w... ...the evening. He spat the last of the midges black
from the back of... ...and wiped them from his eyes.

He walked thro[ugh] ...en that talked to him, although it advised him to
go back, told him ...ng of Dreams should not be idly sought out,
and that he shoul[d] ...d the garden and walking paths, and sit beside
its sweet waters: ...as the garden spoke to him the monk could
never have expl...

He left the g... ...just now he walked on.

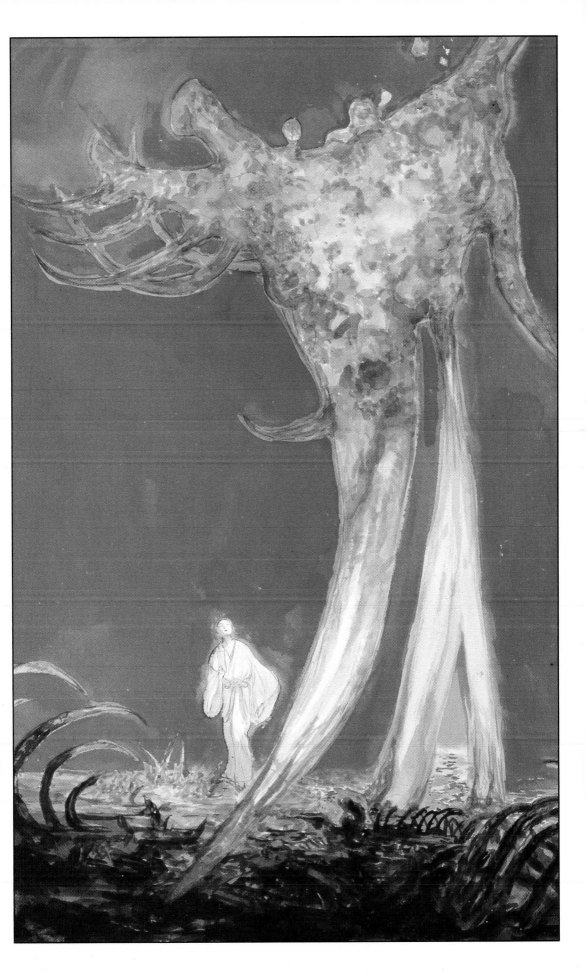

He saw that he was standing in front of two houses, next to each other, and there were two men sitting in the veranda of one of the houses, fishing with lines in the pond below.

"I seek the King of All Night's Dreaming," called the monk. "Am I going the right way?"

"How can you not go to him?" asked the first of the men. "When all the ways are his?"

The second man, who was fat and seemed sad, said nothing.

The monk unfolded his token to show it to them. And it was then, if he had had any doubt before, that he knew for certain that he was dreaming. For he could read the characters on the paper he carried. They were simple characters, so simple he thought it a wonder he had not been able to read them before, and they described one who shaped, who moulded and formed things from chaos and from nothing, who transmuted things from formlessness and shapelessness into that-which-was-not-real, but without which the real would have no meaning.

The second man sneezed, to attract the monk's attention, and then he pointed, almost as if accidently, to a specific hill.

The monk bowed his thanks, and walked toward the hill.

Looking back, as he reached the hill, he saw the fat man was now floating, face-down, in the fish pond, and his murderer was looking down at him from the balcony of his house.

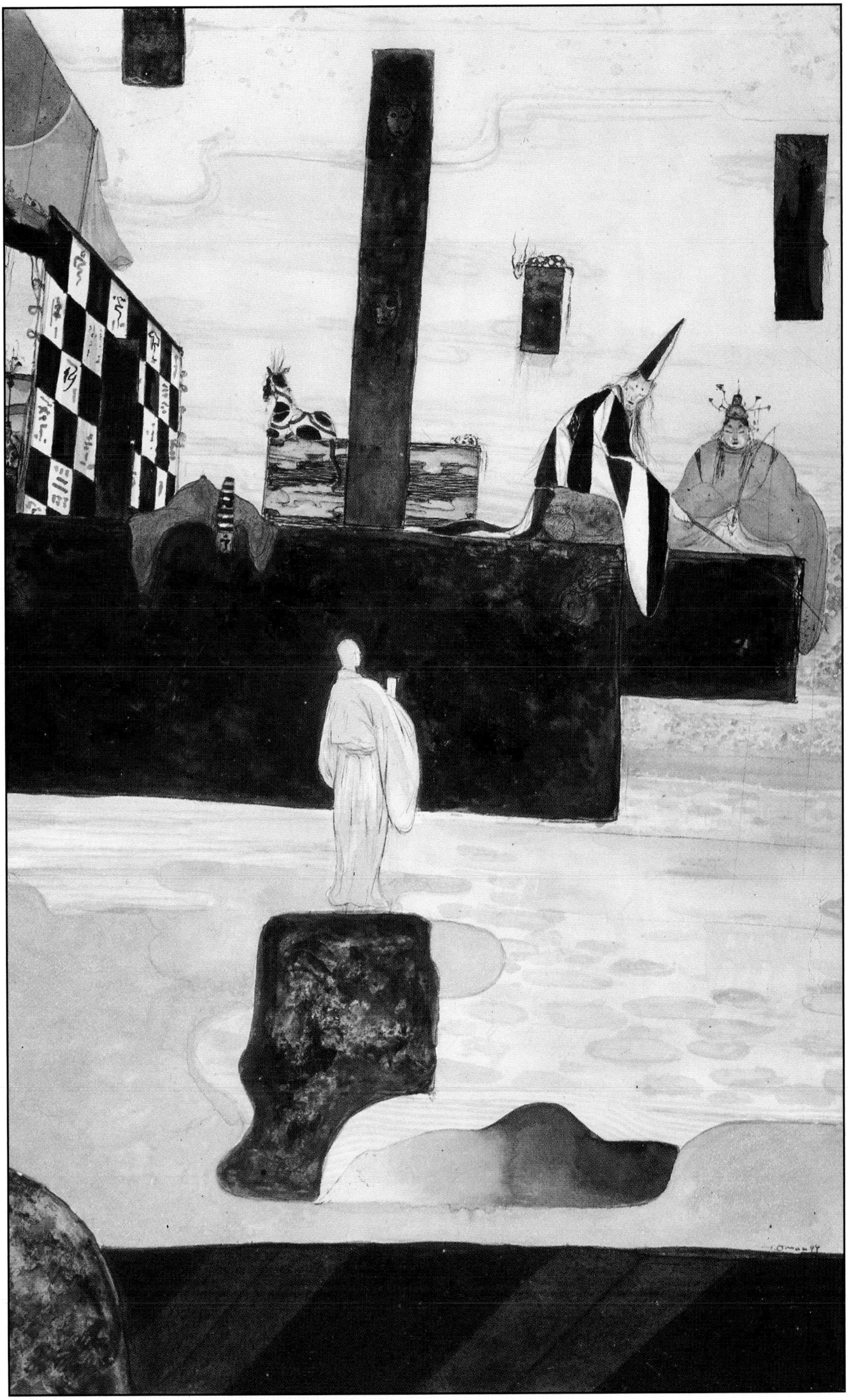

When he was halfway up the hill he looked back one more time and saw that the house had gone, and the men and the pool, and where it had been there was nothing more than a graveyard.

Ahead of him was a huge house, built to be perfectly one with its surroundings: it was at once a shrine and a castle and a home. It was a place of waterfalls and gardens, of painted screens and elegant, curving roofs. He could not tell if it was one house or a hundred houses. He saw courtyards and orchards and trees: spring blossoms and autumn leaves and summer fruit all grew beside each other on the trees of the strange gardens.

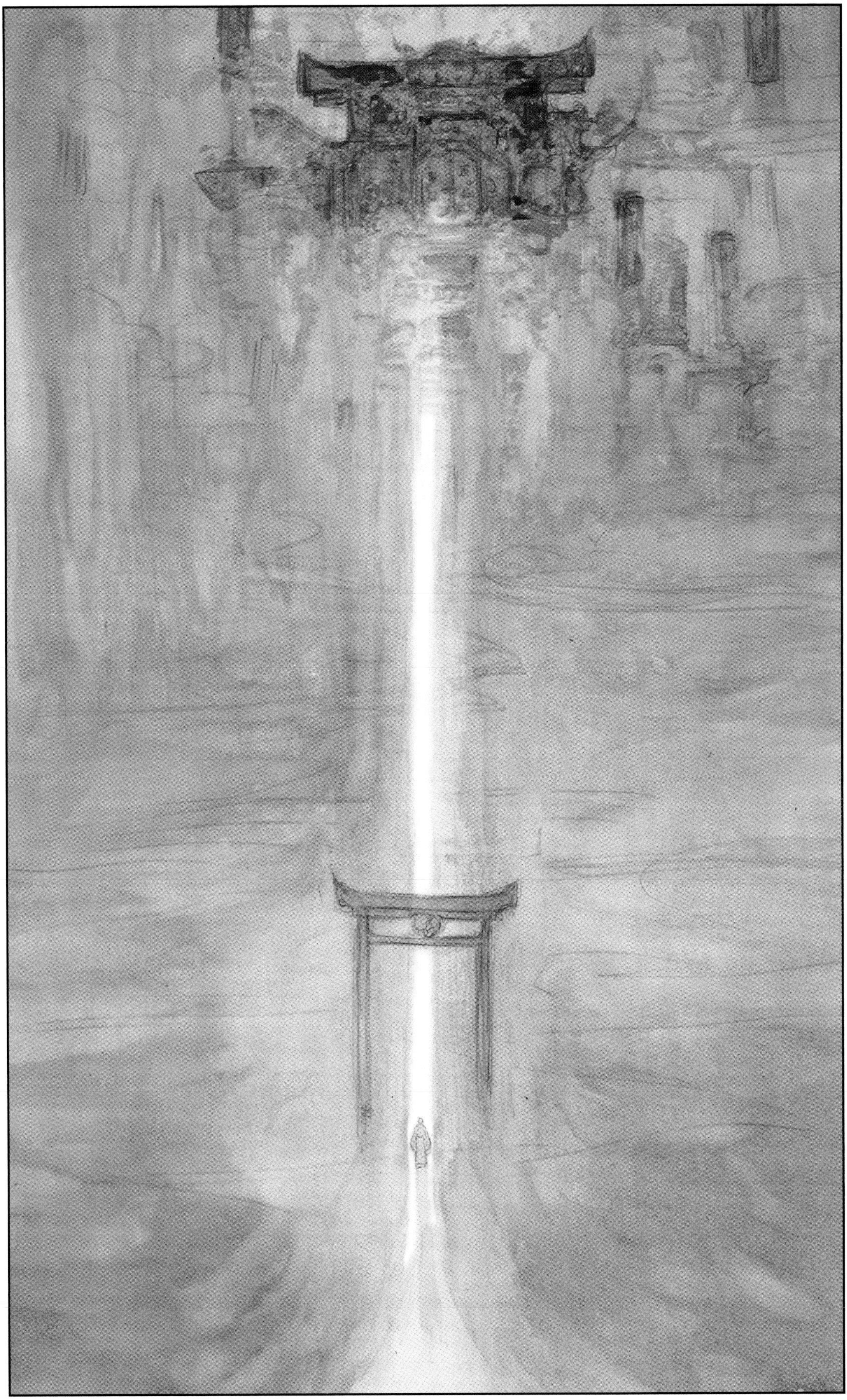

Bright birds sang from those trees; they were of blues and reds so vivid that they seemed like flying flowers, and the songs they sang were passing strange.

The monk had never seen a place like it.

There was a carved gate, made of golden wood, with strange beasts carved upon it, and the monk went to the gate, and beat a small gong that hung there.

The gong was soundless, but he was certain that those who needed to know that he was there knew it.

The gate shifted and *changed*, and a many-coloured creature stood in front of him: a monstrous bird, with a head like a lion's, sharp teeth, a snake's tail, and huge wings. It was an enormous *itsumade*, a creature from legends.

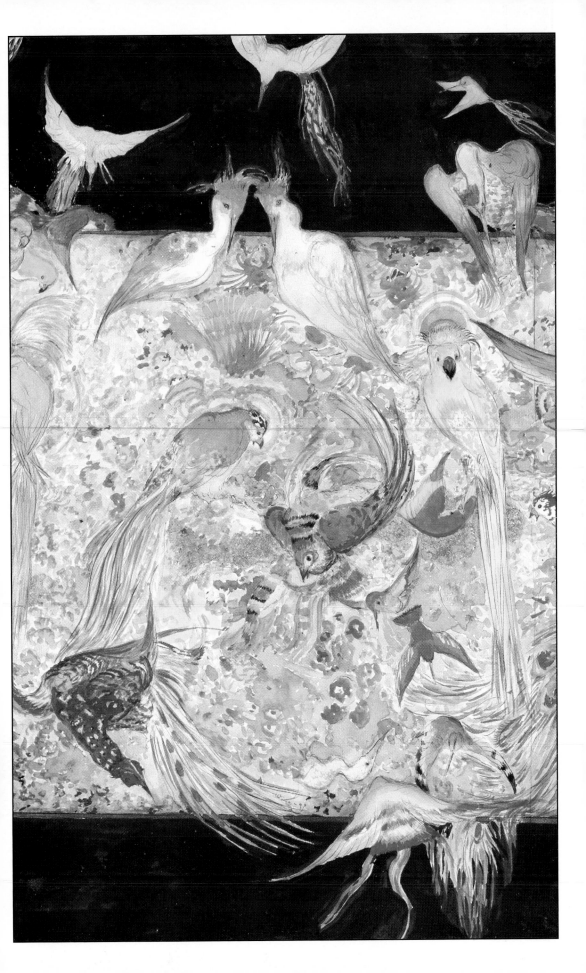

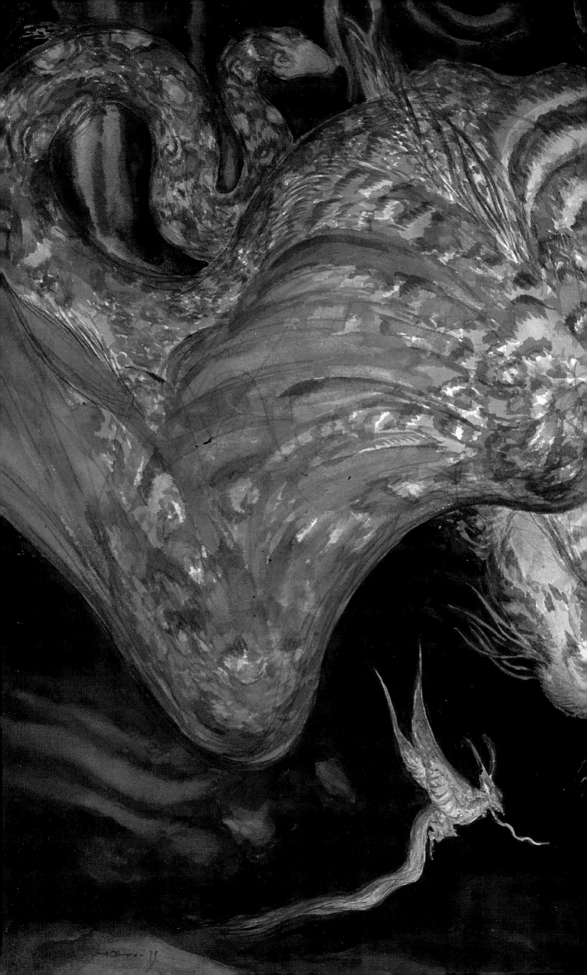

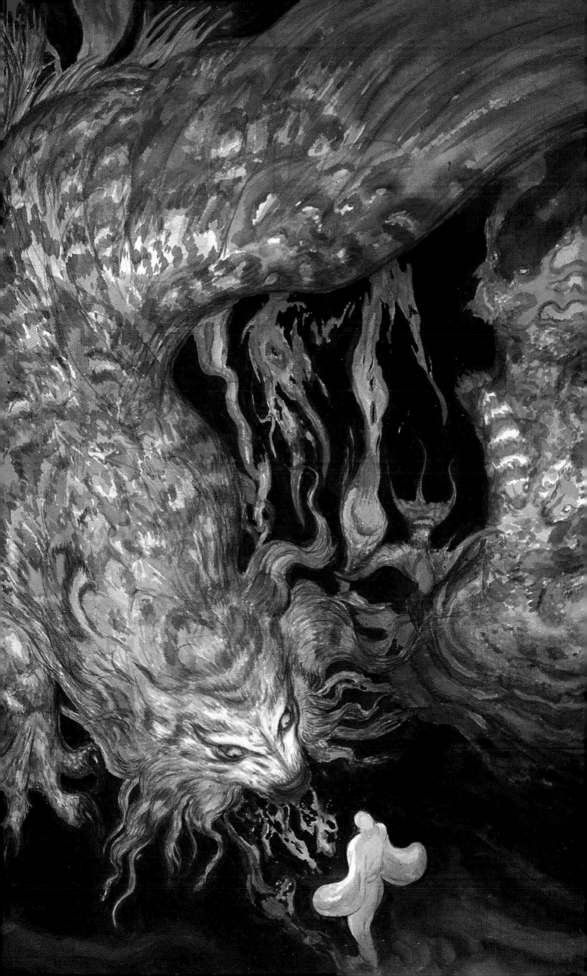

"State your business," said the itsumade. "Who are you, and why do you wish to disturb my master?"

"This place is so beautiful," said the monk, "and its beauty is only increased by knowing that when I wake all other places will be lacking, for they will not be this palace. Do I truly stand in the gardens of the palace of the King of Dreams?"

His words were gentle, but they carried a rebuke to the gatekeeper, for even a monster from legend should remember certain civilities.

"This is indeed the Palace of Dreams," growled the itsumade. "Tell me what you wish, or I shall eat you."

The monk extended his hand, to show the itsumade the slip of paper he had been given. It blazed with its own light. The itsumade lowered its head and grunted. "I did not know," it said. "I thought you were but a dreamer."

The monk became aware at this time that someone was watching him from high in a black pine tree. The watcher was a raven, huge, black and dark, and when it saw that it was observed it flew down to the monk with huge, flapping motions, landing on the path a little way in front of him.

"Follow me," said the raven, in a voice like two stones grinding together.

"Will you take me to the King of Dreams?" asked the monk.

"You would not seek to question a poem, or a falling leaf, or the mist on the mountaintop," said the raven. "Why, then, do you question me?"

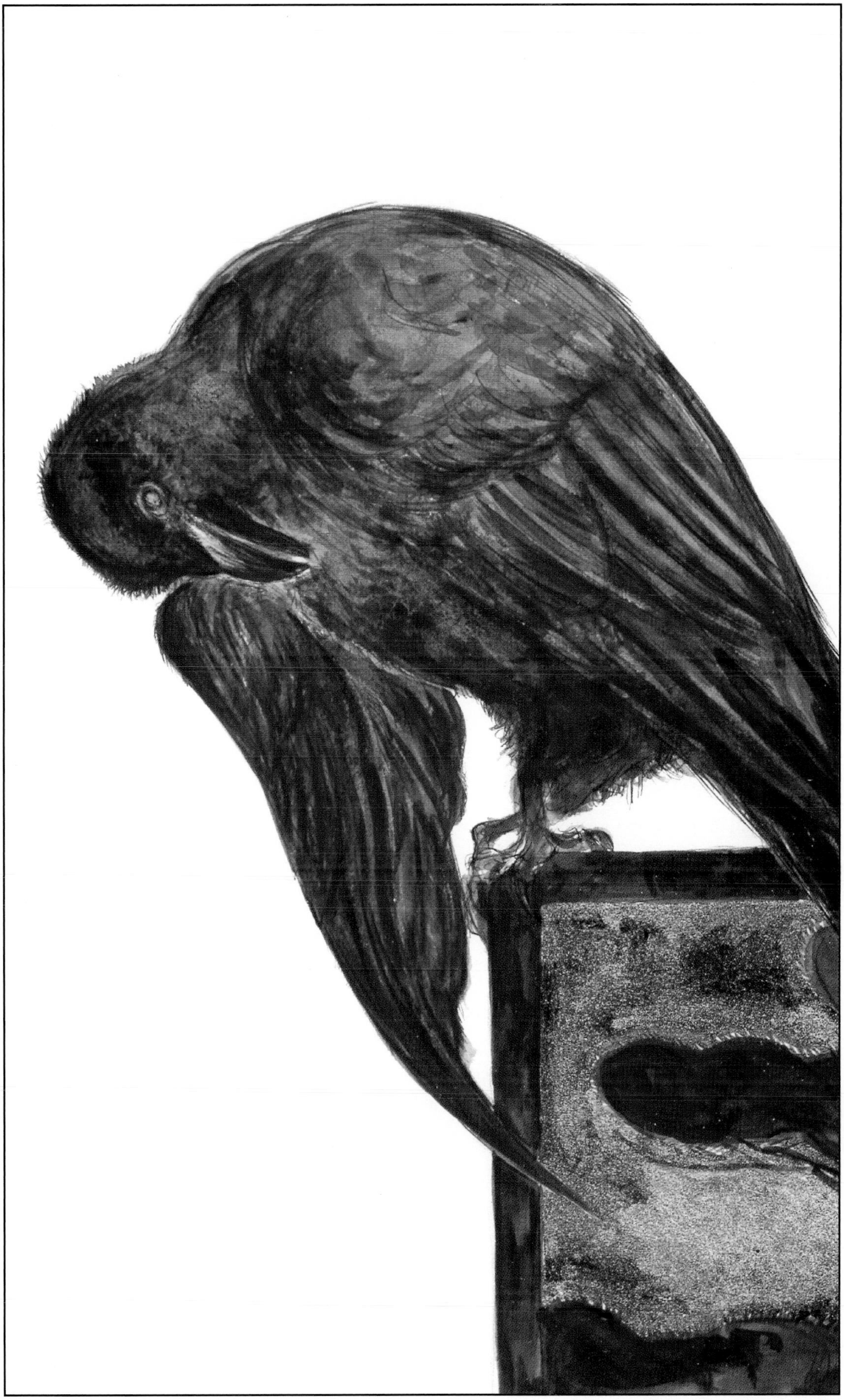

The house was like a maze, and the monk followed the raven through twilit galleries and pavilions, strange and austere; through passages formed of screens, beside calm ponds and perfect rocks and stones they walked, the monk always following the bird.

"From your reply," said the monk, "I presume that you are a poet."

"I serve the King of All Night's Dreaming," said the bird, "and I do his bidding." It flapped its wings and fluttered up, to land on a screen, so it was level with the monk's head. "But you are correct. Once, I was a poet, and, like all poets, I spent too long in the Kingdom of Dreams."

The raven ushered the monk into a room decorated with painted screens. There was a raised dais at one end of the room, and upon the dais sat a wooden chair inlaid with mother-of-pearl. It was a perfect chair, of simplicity and strangeness, and the monk knew that this must be the throne of the King of Dreams.

"Wait here," said the raven; then it strutted from the room like a proud old courtier.

The monk stood nervously in the throne room, and he waited for the arrival of the King of Dreams.

In the monk's imagination, the King of Dreams became an old man, with a long beard and fingernails, and then he looked like the Buddha Amida, and then he became a demon, half man and half dragon.

His eye was caught by the painted screens that bounded the room. As long as he looked at them they remained frozen and still, but when he took his eyes away and looked back he would see things he had not seen before. Creatures would have moved, when he looked away. Tales would end, and new tales begin.

One moment he was alone in the throne room, eyeing the painted screens, and then he was no longer alone, and the King of Dreams sat in the chair upon the dais.

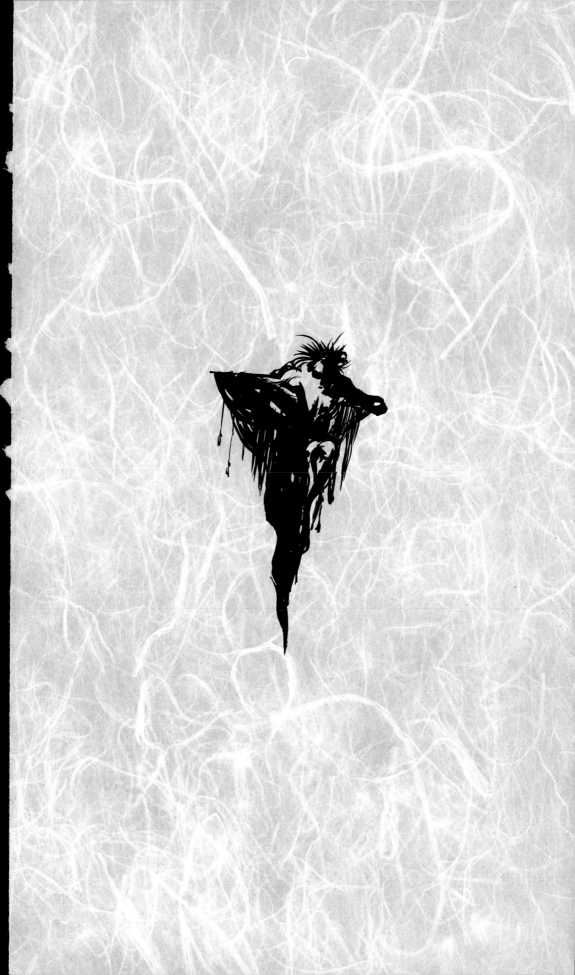

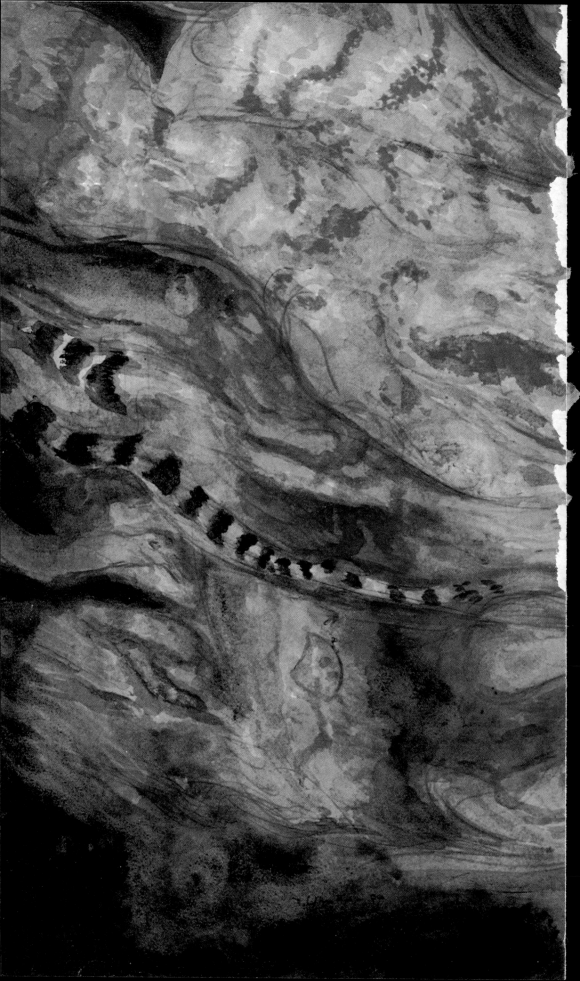

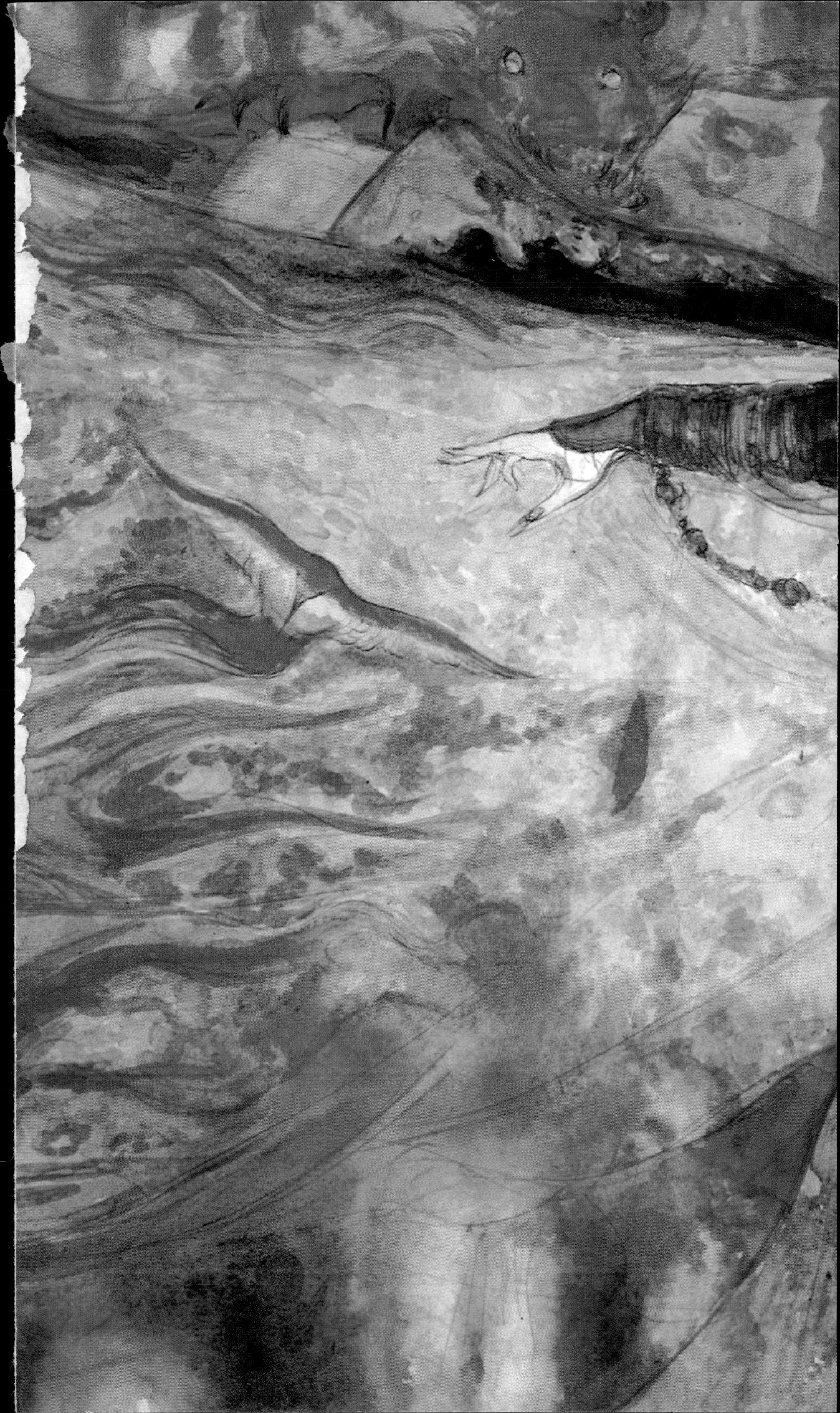

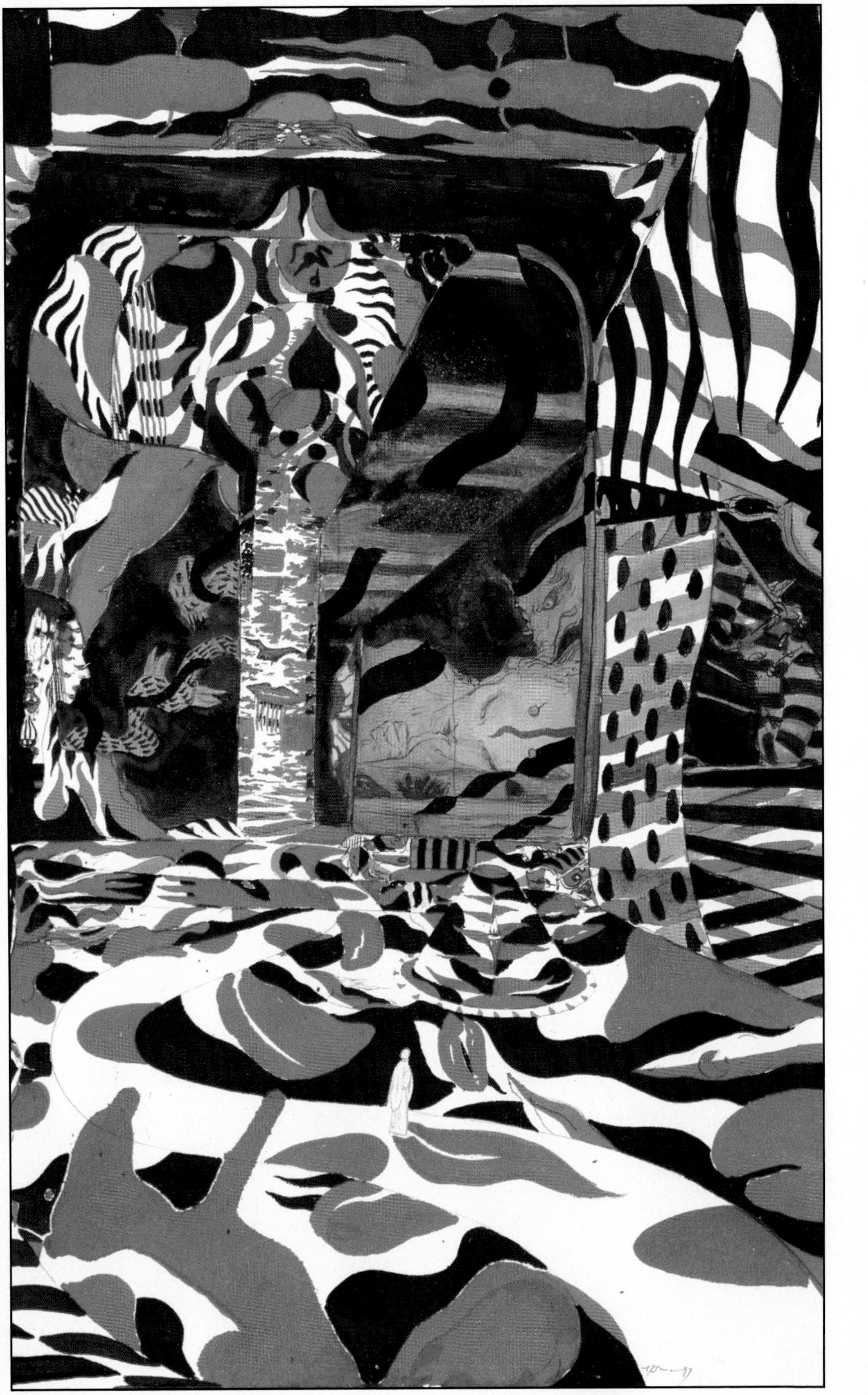

The monk bowed low.

The King of Dreams had skin as pale as the winter moon and hair as black as a raven's wing, and his eyes were pools of night inside which distant stars glittered and burned. His robe was the colour of night, and flames and faces appeared in the base of it and were gone. He began to speak, in a voice that was gentle, yet as strong as silk. *You are welcome in this place,* he said, in words that the monk heard inside his head. *But you should not be here.*

"I have come," said the monk, "to plead for the life of a fox, who is, in my world, lost in dreams. Without your aid, she will perish."

And perhaps that is what she wants, said the King of All Night's Dreaming. *To be lost in dreams. Certainly she has a reason for what she has done, and it is a reason you know little of. Besides, she is a fox. What is her fate to you?*

The monk hesitated. "The Buddha taught us to have love and reverence for all living things. This fox has done me no harm."

The King of Dreams looked the monk up and down. *And that is all?* he said, unimpressed. *That is why you desert your temple, and come to me? Because you love and revere all living things?*

"I have a duty to all things," said the monk. "For, as a monk, I have put behind me all the bonds of desire, all worldly ties."

The King of Dreams said nothing. He seemed to be waiting.

The monk lowered his head, "But I remember the touch of her skin, when she pretended to be a woman, and it is a memory I shall take to my grave, and beyond the grave. And the ties of affection are very hard to break."

I see, said the King of Dreams. He stood, then, and stepped off the dais. He was a very tall man, if he was a man. *Follow me,* he said.

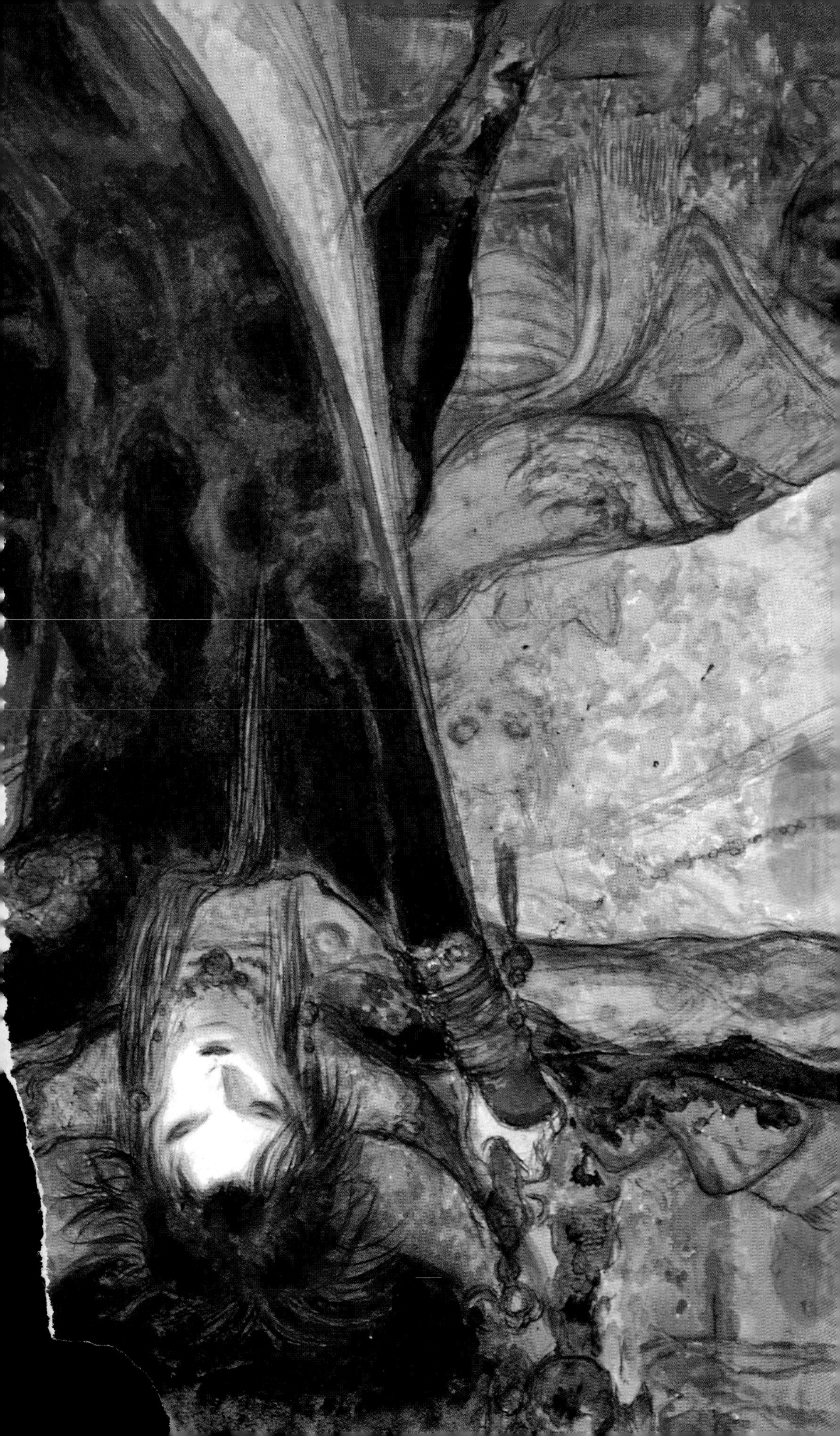

Why would you bring her back? asked the King of Dreams. *It is not what she wants, and it will not bring you happiness.*

The monk said nothing.

The King pointed to the table in the summer house. On it there was a small lacquer box, which the monk recognised from his dreams. There was a key in the lock.

She is in there. Follow her, if that is what you wish.

The monk reached down, and, slowly, he opened the box. It opened, and opened, until it filled the entire world, and, with no hesitation, the monk went inside.

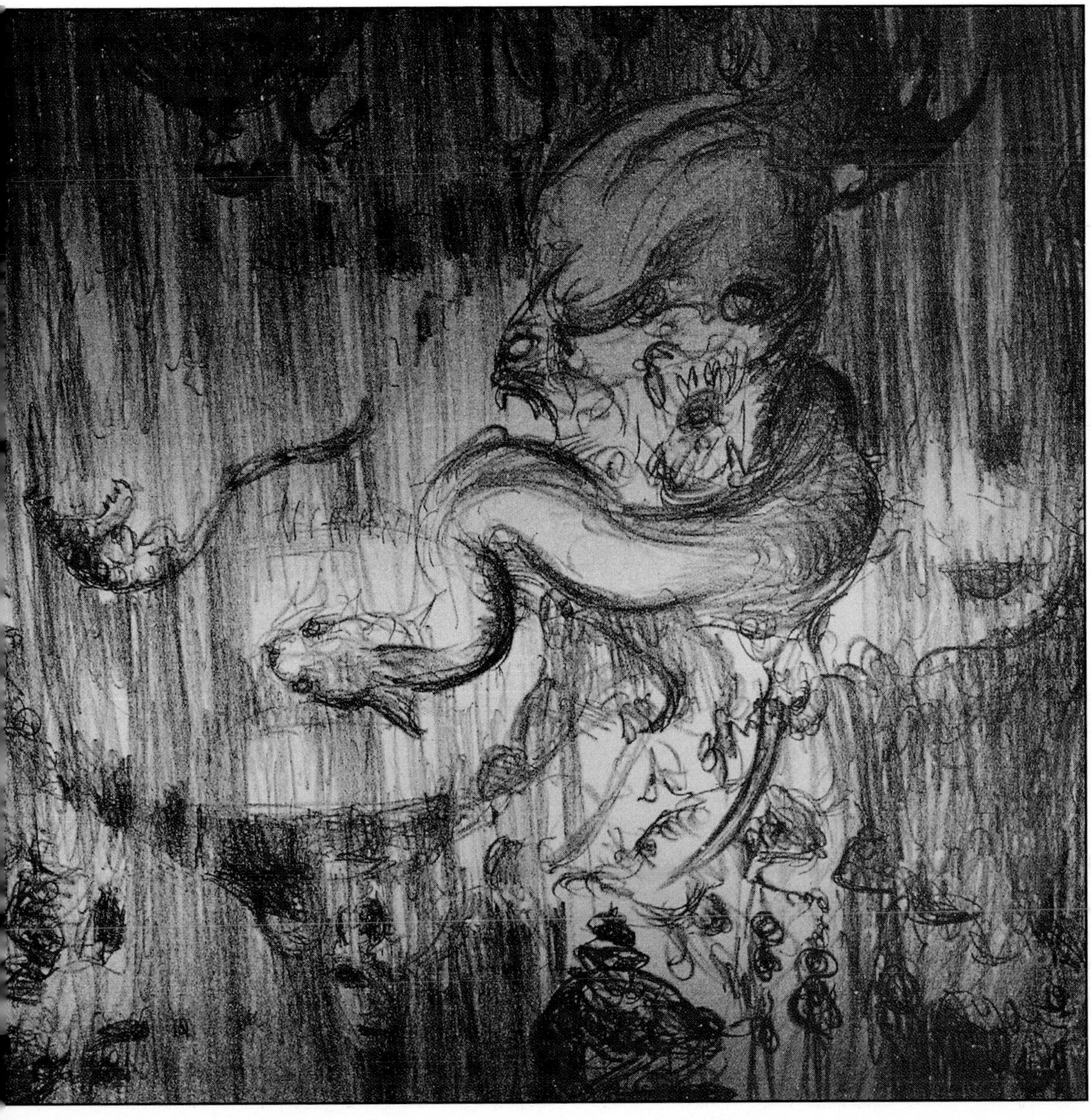

Chapter six

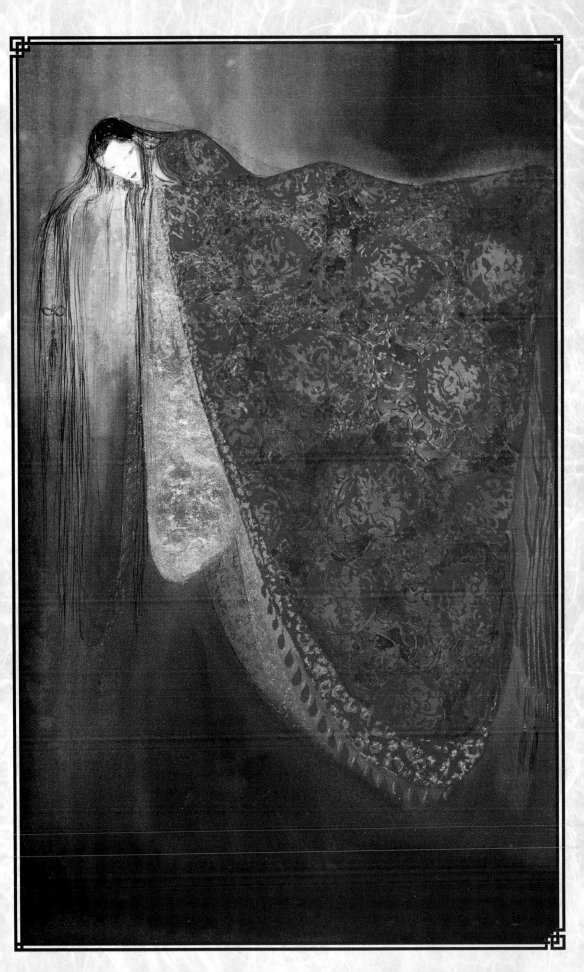

At first it seemed to the monk that the inside of the lacquer box was a familiar place that he had somehow forgotten — perhaps his room as a boy, or a secret room in the temple that had remained hidden until this moment.

There was nothing in the room but a mirror in one corner. From the mirror came a gentle glow, as of sunlight in the final moments of the day.

The monk picked up the mirror.

On the back of the mirror was a painting. It showed two men: one was a fierce, proud man with hunted eyes and a grey beard. The other figure was clearly intended to be the monk himself, although it was covered with stains and mould.

He turned the mirror over, and looked into its face.

He saw a green-eyed girl who seemed almost as if she was painted out of light. When she observed him looking at her, her face fell.

"Why did you come here?" she whispered, sadly. "I gave my life for you."

"You were asleep at the threshold of the door," he told her. "I could not wake you."

She tossed her head. "I hunted the Baku," she told him. "I went to the place where the Baku go, and went with them as they ate dreams, and I entered your dreams as you dreamed them. I was there with you when your father gave you the chest, and as you woke I kept the chest, and when your grandfather gave you the key, I took it from you as you woke.

"Through all the next day I followed you, and when night came I lay down at your door, in the place that the dream would have to come on its way to you, and I slept. I saw the dream slipping through the darkness, and I sprang upon it, and made it my own. And in my dream I opened the chest with a key, and it opened, huge as the sky, and I had no choice but to enter.

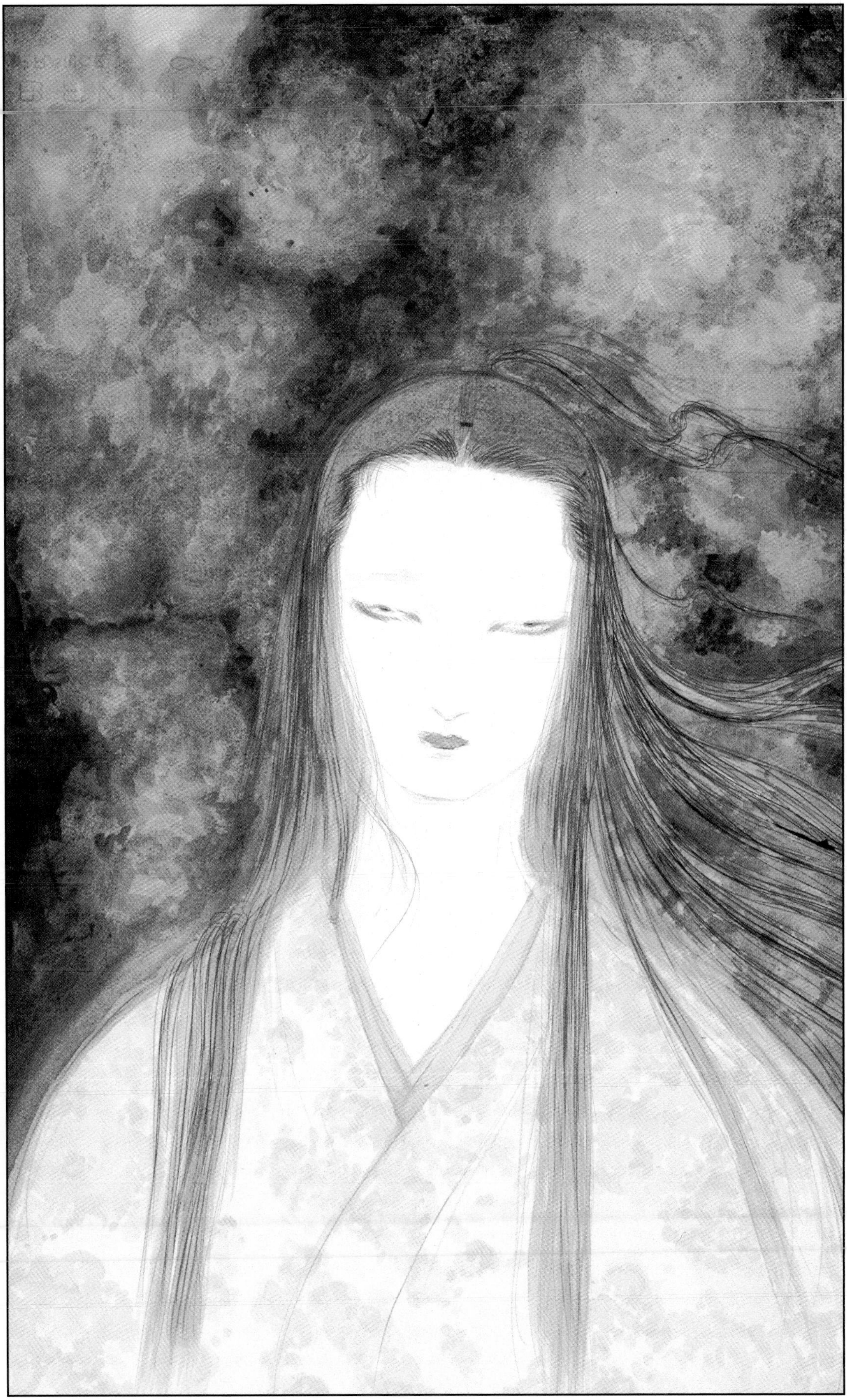

"And then I was very afraid, for I was lost in this box, and I could not find my way out again. I had lost the path that would take me back to my body. I was sad and scared, but also I was proud, for I knew that I had saved your life."

"Why would you do this for me?" asked the monk, although he knew already that he understood why she had done it.

The fox spirit girl smiled. "Why did you search me out?" she asked. "Why did you come here?"

"Because I care for you," he said.

She lowered her eyes. "Then — now you have come here, and now you have

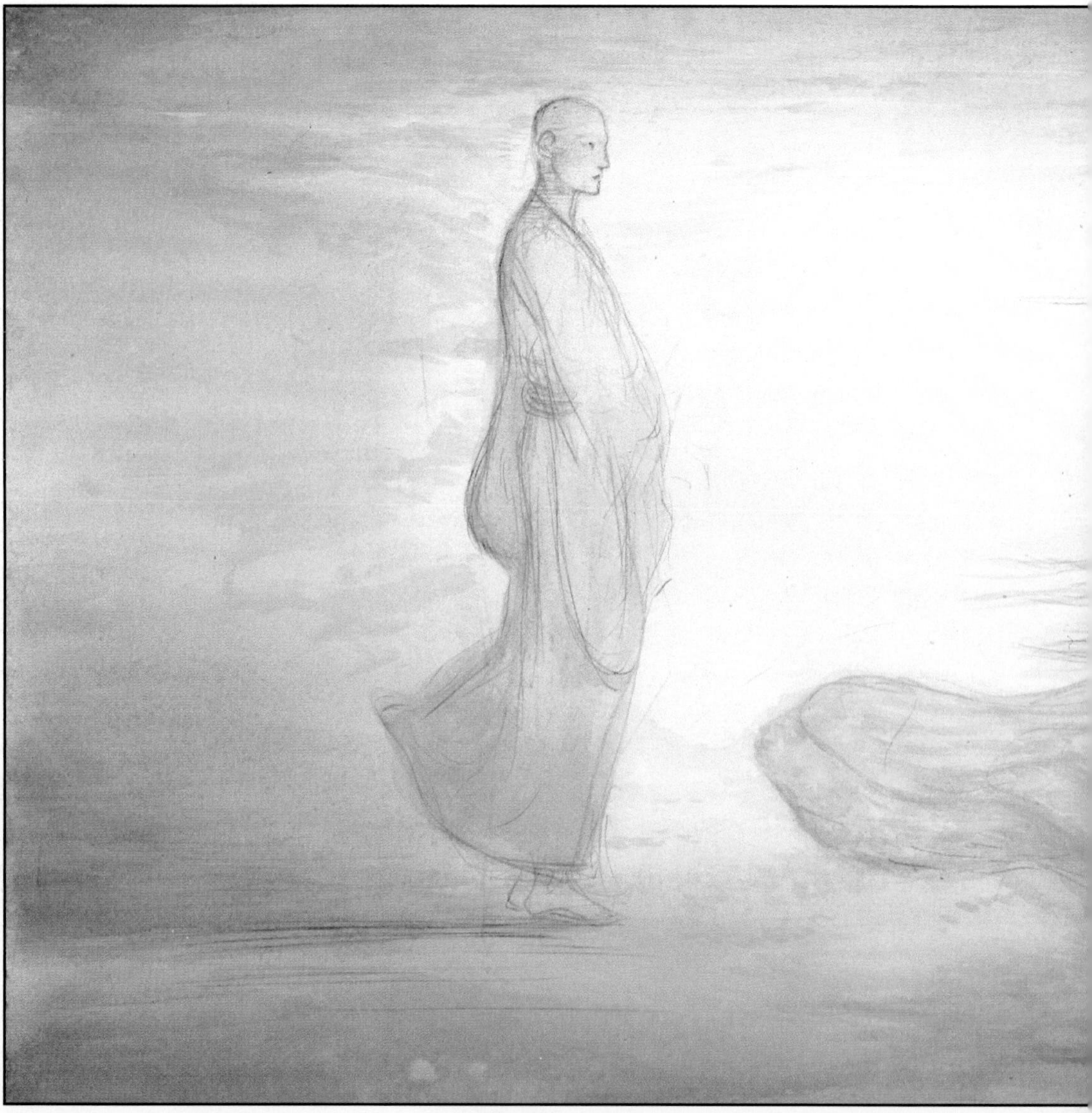

learned the truth — you must know that it is time for you to leave. I have saved your life. The onmyoji who is your enemy will die in your place, and you can return to your temple, grow your pumpkins and your silly dry yams, and, when it is appropriate, say a prayer for me."

"I have come to free you," said the monk. "It is my task."

"And how would you free me?" asked the girl, sadly. "Can you break the metal of the mirror?"

"No," said the monk. "I can not." And he pronounced the name that had been written on the slip of paper that Binzuru Harada had given him on the bridge. Standing beside him was the King of Dreams.

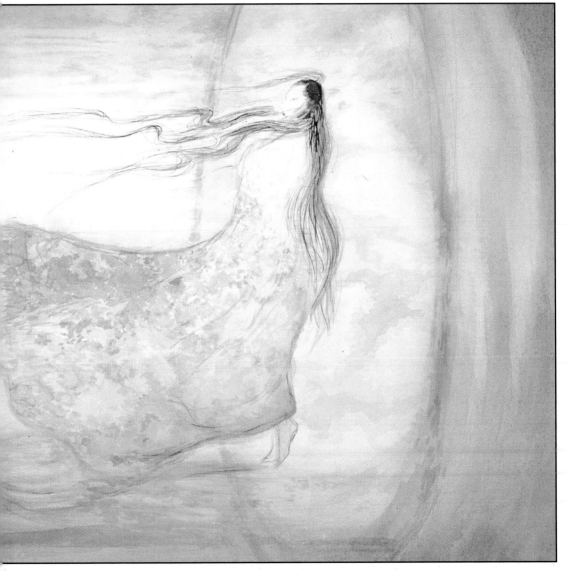

Well, said the king, *are you ready to leave this place?*

"My lord," said the monk. "I am a monk. I own nothing but my begging bowl. But the dream that fox dreamed was my dream by rights. I ask for it to be returned to me."

But, said the king, *if I return your dream to you, you must die in her place.*

"I understand that," said the monk. "But it is my dream. And I will not have this fox die in my place."

The King of Dreams nodded. His face did not change, but it seemed to the monk that he was saddened by this, but that he was also pleased, and the young monk knew that his request had been the correct one.

The king gestured, and the mirror lay empty on the floor, while the fox spirit stood beside the monk in the dark.

You have done the right thing, at some cost to yourself, said the king to the monk. *So I shall, in my turn, do something for you. You may have a little time to say farewell to the fox.*

The fox spirit threw herself to the floor at the king's feet. "But you swore to help me!" she said, angrily.

And I helped you.

"It is not *fair,*" said the fox.

No, agreed the king. *It is not.*

And, calmly and imperceptibly, he left the two of them alone in that place.

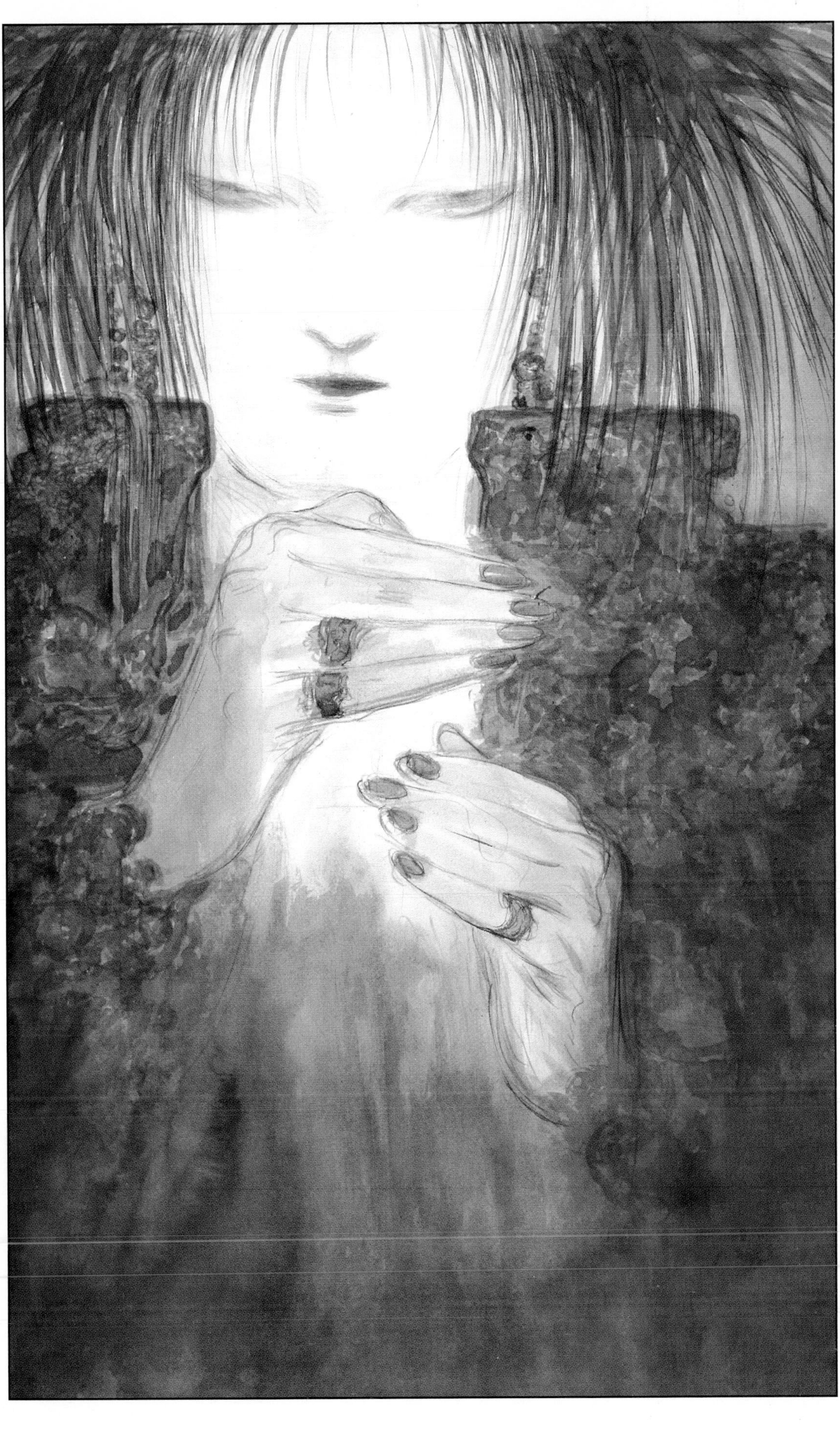

That is all the tale tells us of this moment: that he left them alone to bid each other farewell. Perhaps they said formal farewells, awkwardly, the space between them — between a man who had forsaken the world and a fox spirit — a gulf that could not be crossed. It is certainly possible.

But one remembers all they had done, one for the other, and one might conjecture that, at this time, they made love. Or that they dreamed that they did.

Perhaps.

When they were done with all their farewells, the King of Dreams rejoined them.

Now all will be as it should be, he said, and the monk found himself staring out from the mirror at the fox.

"I would have given my life for you," she whispered, sadly.

"Live," said the monk.

"You shall be revenged," said the fox. "The onmyoji who did this to you will learn what it means to take something from a fox."

The monk looked at the fox-girl from the mirror. "Seek not revenge, but the Buddha," he said to her. Then he turned, and walked into the heart of the mirror, and he was gone.

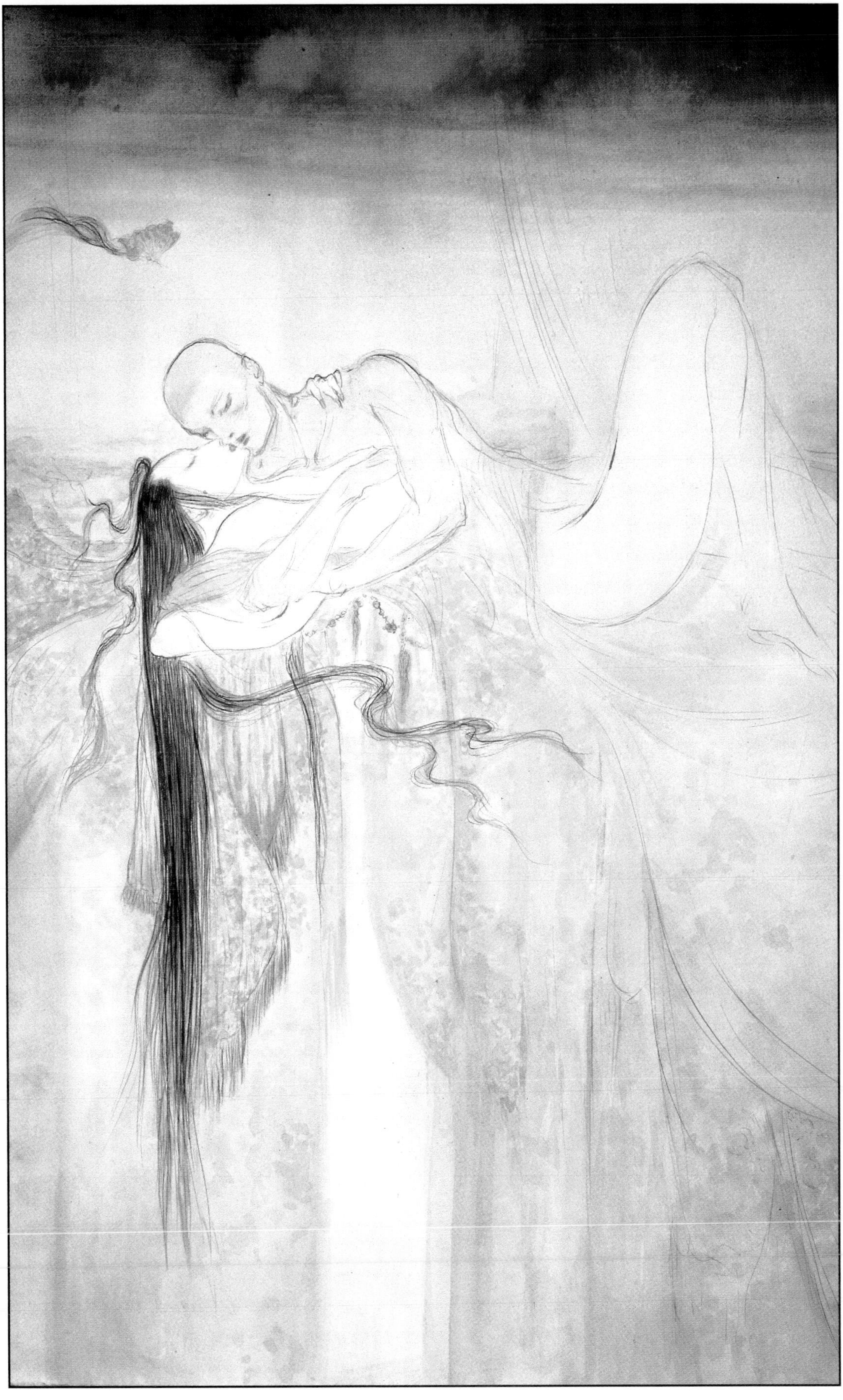

The fox sat in the wilderness of rocks beside the huge black fox of dreams.

"All that I did," she said, "everything I tried to do. All for nothing."

Nothing is done entirely for nothing, said the fox of dreams. *Nothing is wasted. You are older, and you have made decisions, and you are not the fox you were yesterday. Take what you have learned, and move on.*

"Where is he now?" she asked.

His body is on his sleeping mat in the temple. His spirit will go where it is meant to go.

"So he will die," she said.

Yes, he said.

"He told me not to seek revenge, but to seek the Buddha," said the fox spirit, sadly.

Wise counsel, said the fox of dreams. *Vengeance can be a road that has no ending. You would be wise to avoid it. And...?*

"I shall seek the Buddha," said the fox, with a toss of her head. "But first I shall seek revenge."

As you will, said the fox of dreams, and the fox could not tell if he was happy or sad, satisfied or dissatisfied.

And with a switch of his tail he bounded away across the landscape of dreams, and left the little fox more alone than she had ever been.

She woke in the little temple on the side of the mountain, beside the body of the monk. His eyes were closed, and his breath was shallow, and his skin was the colour of sea-foam.

It hurt, having already said goodbye to him, to have him still there. But she stayed with him, and attended to his body.

He died, peacefully, on the following day.

There was a funeral for him, in the little temple, and he was buried on the mountainside, beside the other monks who had tended the little temple in the centuries that had gone before.

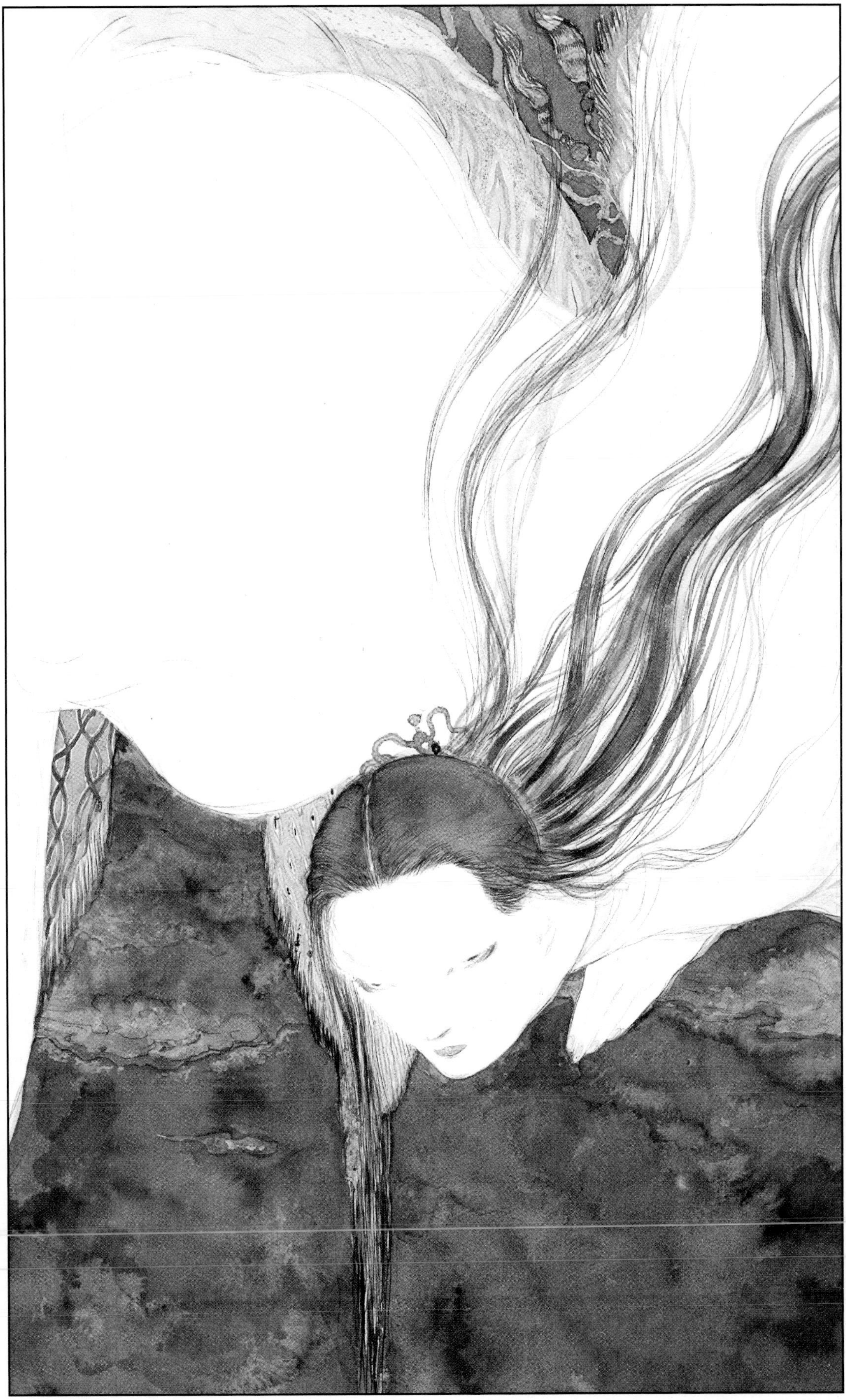

The full of the moon came and went, and the waning moon rode high in the sky, and the Master of Yin-Yang was still alive. And more than that, he could feel his fear dying within him.

He took the lacquer box, the black key, and the little porcelain plates, and he wrapped them up in the square of silk (which showed only his face now, for of the other painted figure there was nothing more than the shadow of a stain) and, at the dead of night, he buried them beneath the roots of a tree that had long ago been struck by lightning and was twisted into a most disturbing shape.

He was relieved that he was alive. He was happier than he had ever been. Those were good days for the onmyoji.

The moon was again full in the sky when he was visited by a maiden of high birth, who wished to consult him about propitious days. A mist hung heavy in the air that day, and it twined its tendrils through the onmyoji's house.

She paid for his wisdom with gold coins so old they were almost featureless, and with rice of the finest quality. Then she left his house, in a magnificent ox-drawn carriage.

The Master of Yin-Yang told a servant to follow her on horseback, and to discover who the maiden was, and where she lived.

Several hours later, the servant returned. He said that the maiden lived in an old but impressive house, several *ri* north of Kyoto, and described the area to the onmyoji.

Days passed. The onmyoji could not get the maiden's face out of his mind, nor the way she walked, respectful and seductive at the same time. He imagined possessing her, touching her, owning her.

When he closed his eyes at night the maiden was there: her hair, so long, and so very black; her eyes, the shade of green leaves uncurling in the spring sunlight, her feet, which moved like tiny mice; the delicacy of her hand upon her fan; her voice, like a song heard in a dream.

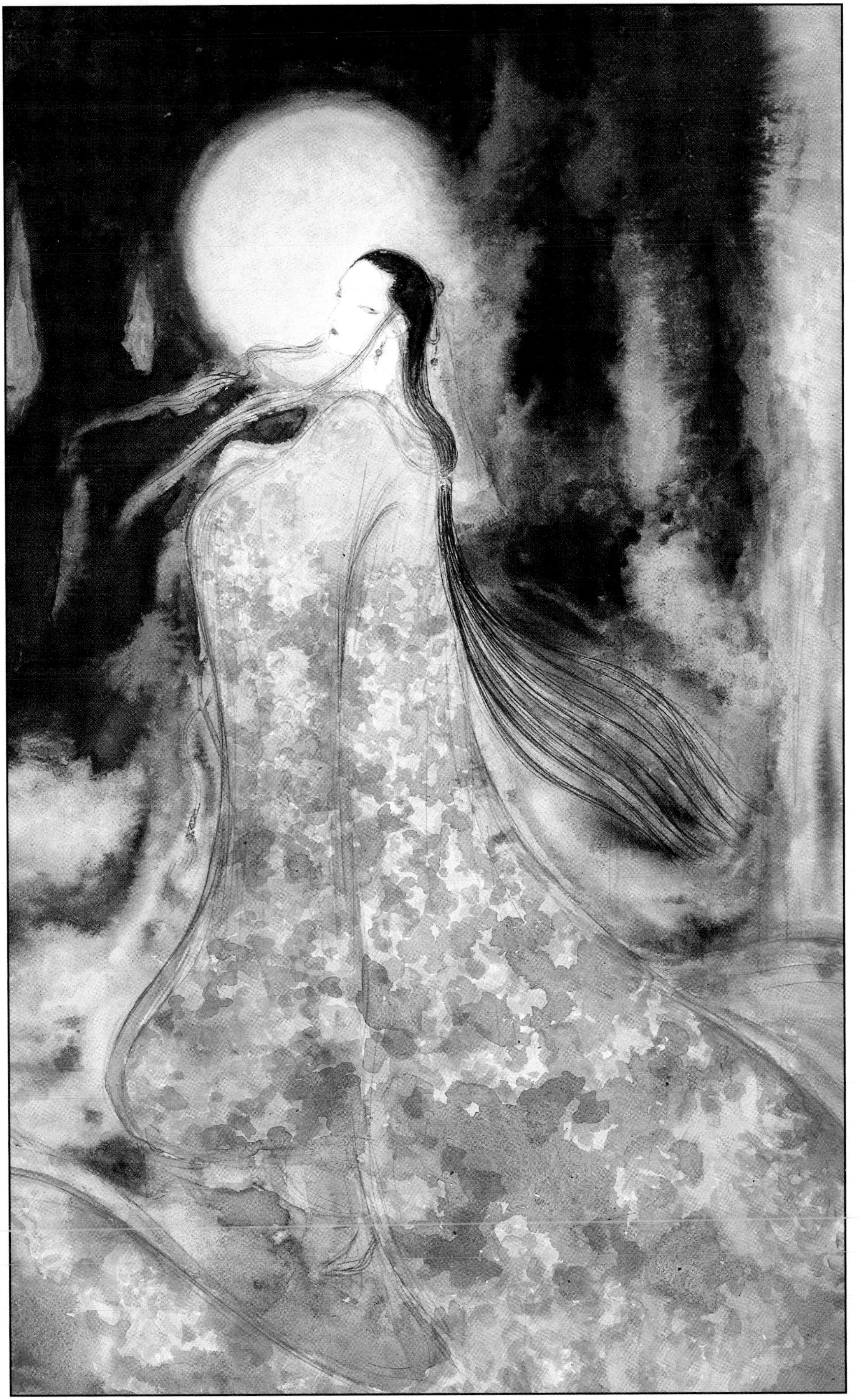

When he went to make love to his concubine, he found she did not interest him, and he returned to his room, where he wrote a poem comparing his feelings about the maiden to the autumn wind, stirring the surface of a pool that had, until now, been placid, and he gave it to the servant to take to the maiden.

The servant brought back her reply, a poem in which she spoke of the reflection of the moon in the pool stirred by the wind. His heart swelled within him when he read it, astonished by the grace and ease of her brushwork.

He asked his oracles about her. The old woman laughed at him, cackling so hard he thought that she would die, and said nothing. The young woman with the cold hands said, "The man she loved is dead."

"Good," said the onmyoji. "When is the most propitious day to visit her?"

But at that the three women all giggled and laughed as if they were mocking him, and angrily he left their house.

On the following evening he arrived at the maiden's house. He begged her pardon for his arrival, claiming that he was forced, by knowledge gained from his divinations, to leave his house travelling to the north, which was an auspicious direction, and that he needed to stay overnight in the north before leaving in the morning for the city.

She invited him to dine with her.

The house was magnificent. He and the maiden dined alone, and through the evening her servants brought them the finest foods he had ever eaten.

"I have never tasted anything this fine!" he said, nibbling some exotic meat in a cold sauce.

"And to think," she said, "if I had not been here, you might have been forced to sit in the tumbledown ruins of an old and empty house, and to dine upon mice and spiders."

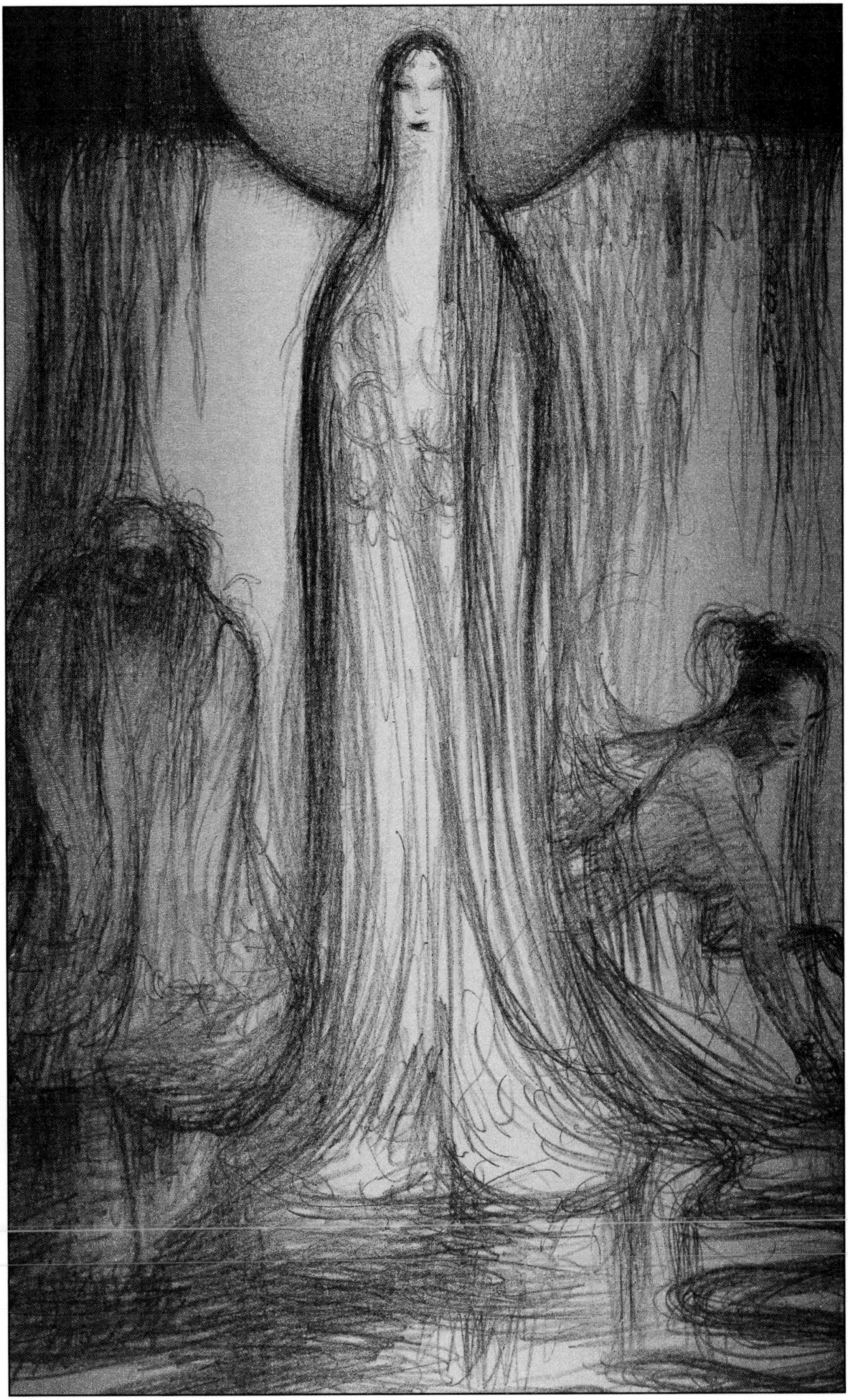

At the end of the meal, he made it clear that he would like to enjoy her physical favours. She poured them both sake, and told him that it was quite out of the question.

"For why would I wish to be second in your affections?" she asked. "You have a wife. You have a concubine. What would I be?"

"I will be yours, and yours alone," he told her.

"You say that," she said, "but after you have made love to me then your wife and your concubine will seem more attractive, and I will be left alone here. I do not think you should stay the night here. Your carriage will take you to another house for the night. If ever you are free to love me, and me alone, then come back."

"It is as good as done!" he said.

"But I can never be yours," she told him, "while you have your house. For I should want you to come and live in my house, with me. Indeed, my house would be yours, and would be yours forever. But if you had a house, you might sigh after it, and one day you would leave me for your own house." She shifted then, minutely, and the onmyoji imagined he caught the briefest glimpse of the white swell of her breast within her robe.

"I shall take care of my house," said the onmyoji, his mind a single burning flame of lust.

"And there is one more thing," said the maiden, her green eyes burning into his. "And that is your magic. How can I be your love, and your wife, if I knew that you commanded Tengu and Oni, and that in your scrolls you had the knowledge to change me into a bird if I displeased you?"

She bent over to pour him more sake, which caused her robe to fall open a little more, and the onmyoji saw a white breast, tipped by a nipple as pink as the sunset. At this, the onmyoji leapt to grab hold of her but the maiden deftly moved back, avoiding his grasp as if she had barely noticed it, and she bade him goodnight.

When he realised that their time together was over he sighed so loudly it seemed that the hinges of the world were groaning. There was a madness that came on him then, or so they said.

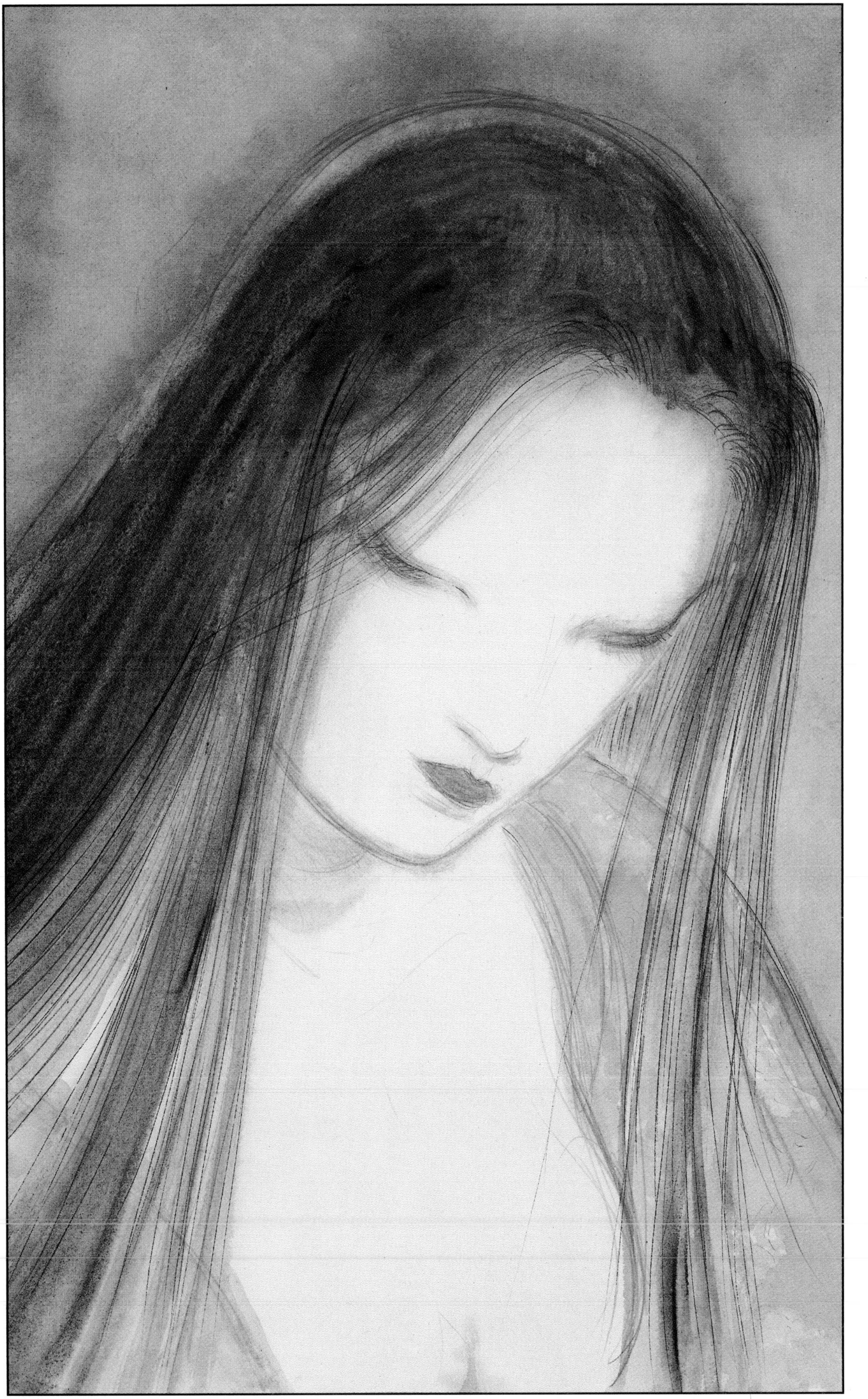

On the following night there were two fires in the city of Kyoto. The first house to burn was that of the onmyoji, the seventeenth-finest house in all the city. He was not suspected of any involvement, having left the house, earlier that day, in a cart loaded high with all his scrolls and his implements of magic. It was a tragic fire, for his wife and his concubine and all his servants were asleep inside the house as it blazed, and it took their lives.

The other house to burn was a hovel on the outskirts of the city, in a neighborhood of ill-repute. It was a house where three women lived, who were said to have been fortunetellers and herbalists. No one knows if they were in the house when it burned, for the only remains that were found in the ashes were the bones and skulls of babes and of small children.

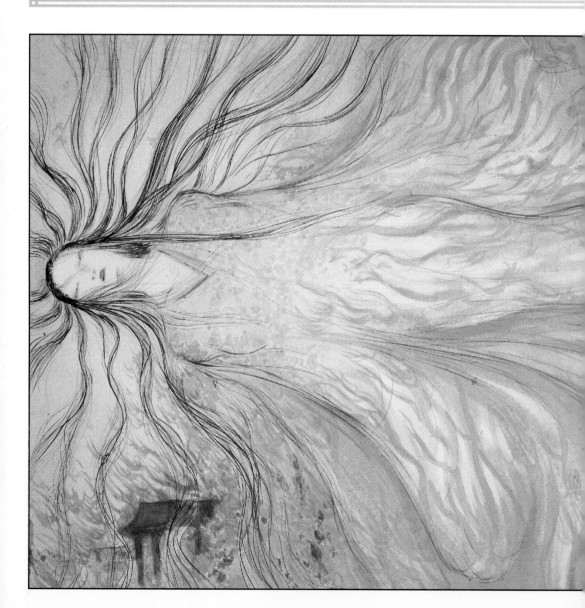

It was evening when the Master of Yin-Yang arrived at the house of the maiden who had won his heart.

"My house is burned," he said, "and my women are dead. I have no one to love but you and nowhere to be but here."

She smiled at him then, a smile of such happiness that it seemed to him that the sun had come out and shone on him alone.

"And in this cart," he told her, "I have my knowledge. All my scrolls, all my magical implements. All the amulets and wands and names that give me power over the spirits and demons, that allow me to tell the future. All of it, I have brought here to lay at your feet."

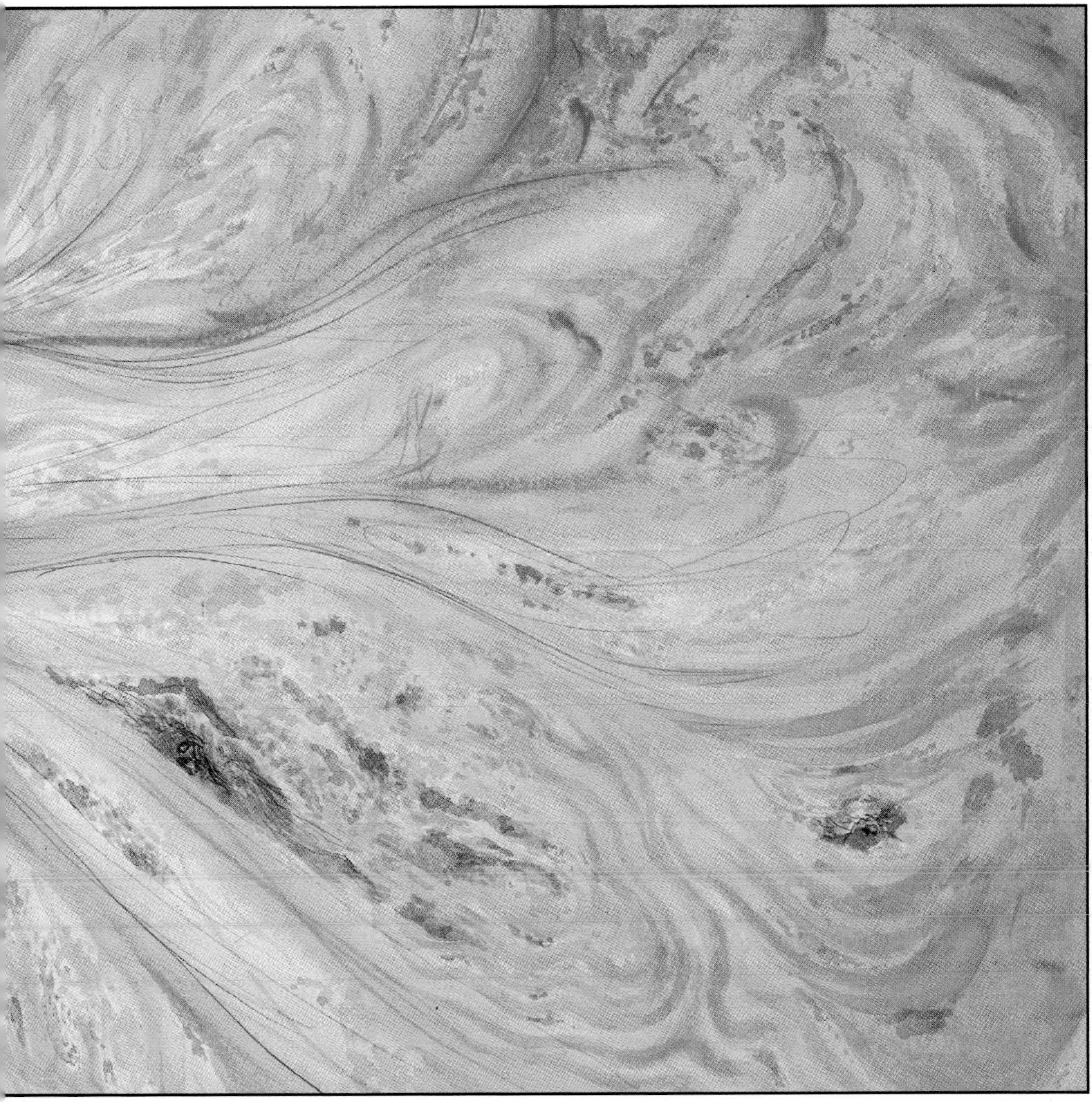

The maiden nodded, and several of her servants took the cart, and unpacked its contents, and took the things he had brought away.

"There," said the onmyoji, "now, I am yours, and there is nothing that can come between us."

"There is still something between us," she told him. "Your robe. Take it off. Let me see you as you are."

The madness and the lust mingled in the onmyoji's veins. He stepped out of his robe and stood there, naked, in the misty twilight. She picked up his robe, and held it.

He opened his arms wide to embrace the maiden.

The maiden stepped closer to him. "Now," she whispered. "You have no house, no wife, no concubine, no magic, no clothing. You have lost it all. And so it is time that I gave something to you."

She reached up her hands to his head, and pulled it close to her lips, as if she were about to kiss him, just above one eye.

"But you shall keep your life," she said, "for he would not have wanted me to kill you."

A fox's teeth are very sharp.

And with a flick of her tail, she was gone.

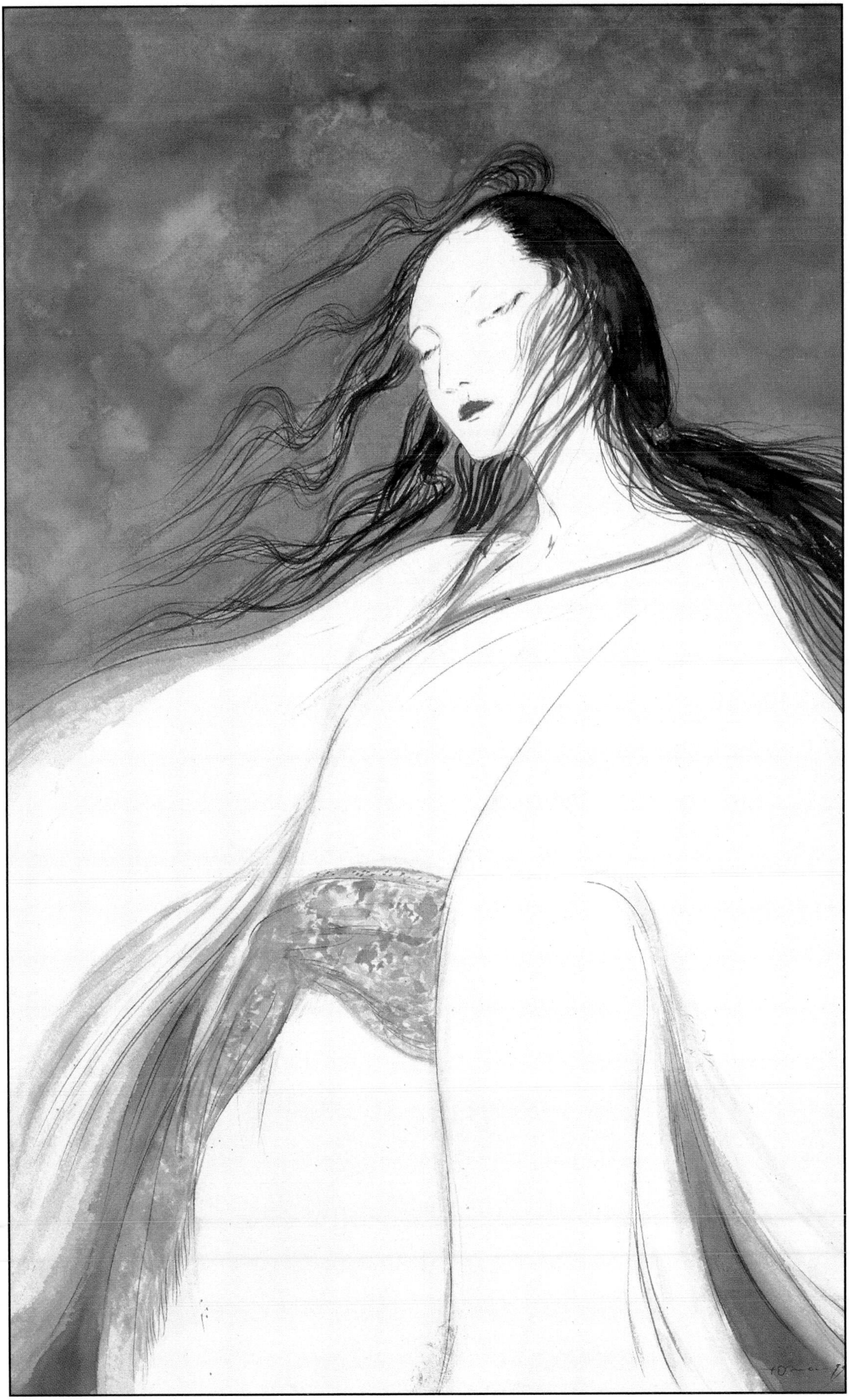

The Master of Yin-Yang was found the next morning in the grounds of a house that had been abandoned twenty years earlier, when the official whose family had owned it was disgraced. Some said it was guilt that had brought him there, for, fifteen years earlier, the onmyoji had been in the service of the lord who had caused the downfall of that family.

He was naked, and ashamed, and quite mad.

Some said it was the loss of his wife and his house in a fire that had driven him to madness. Others claimed it was the loss of his eye, while the superstitious, speaking among themselves, claimed that it was fox magic.

His old associates avoided him in the days that were to come, when they saw him begging in the streets, with only rags to cover his nakedness, only a rag about his head to hide the ruins of his face.

He lived in misery and squalor and madness until he died, with no happiness to be found anywhere in his life, save the momentary happiness of dreams.

But of how he lived, beyond this point, and of how he died, all the tales are silent.

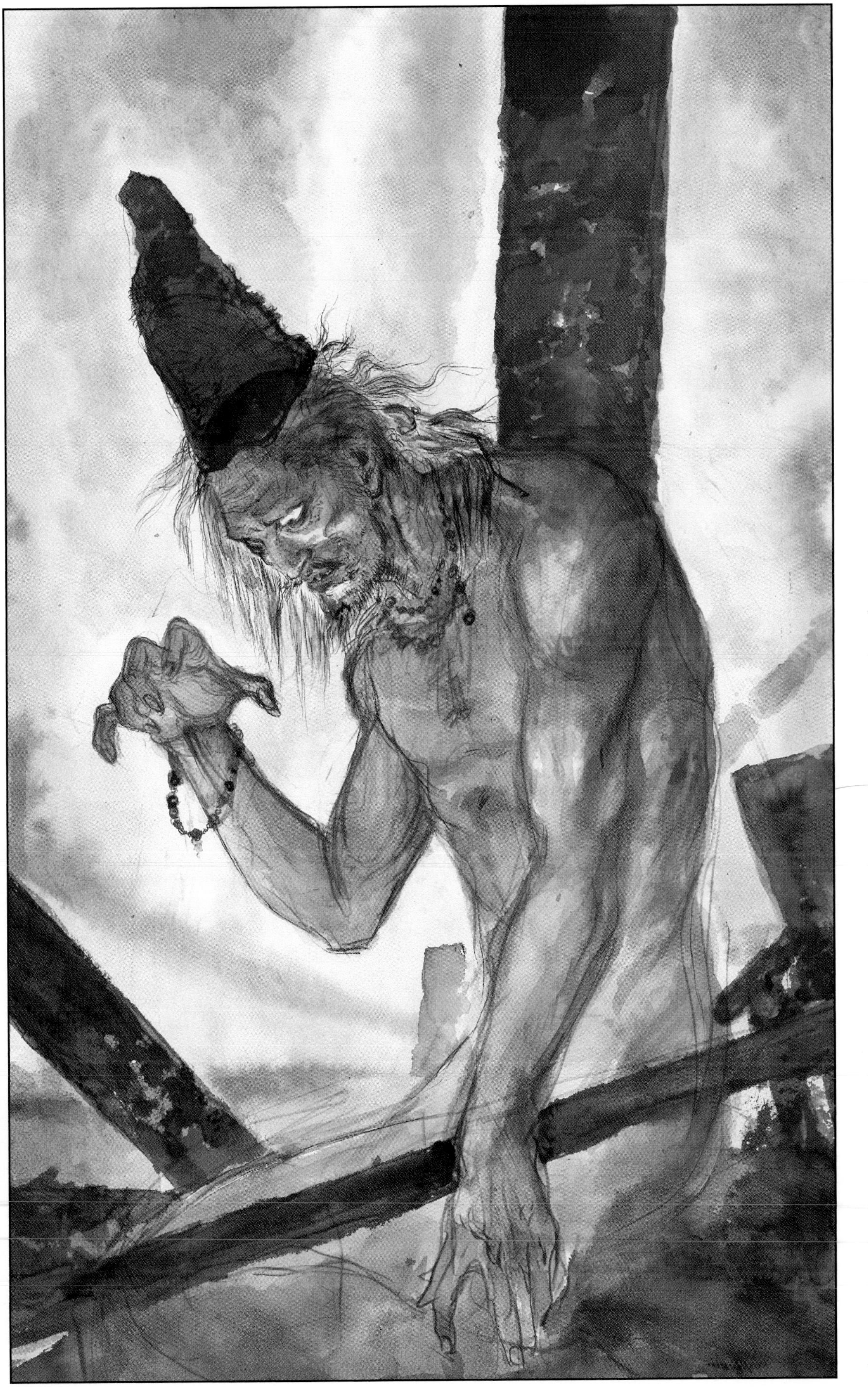

"But what good did it do?" asked the raven.

Good? asked the King of All Night's Dreaming.

"Yes," said the raven. "The monk was to die, and he died. The fox who tried to help him failed to help him. The onmyoji lost everything. What good did it do, your granting her wish?"

The king stared away at the horizon. In his eye a single star glinted and was gone.

Lessons were learned, said the pale king. *Events occurred as it was proper for them to do. I do not perceive that my attention was wasted.*

"Lessons were learned?" said the raven, bristling its neck feathers, and raising its black head high. "By whom?"

By all of them. Particularly the monk.

The raven croaked once in the back of its throat, and hopped from one foot to the other. It appeared to be hunting for words. The king watched it patiently with dark eyes. "But he is *dead*," said the raven, after some time.

Come to that, so are you, my raven, but there were lessons in here for you as well.

"And did you also learn a lesson?" asked the raven, who had once been a poet.

But the pale king chose not to answer and remained wrapped in silence, staring at the horizon; and after some time the raven flapped heavily away into the sky of dreams, and left the king entirely alone.

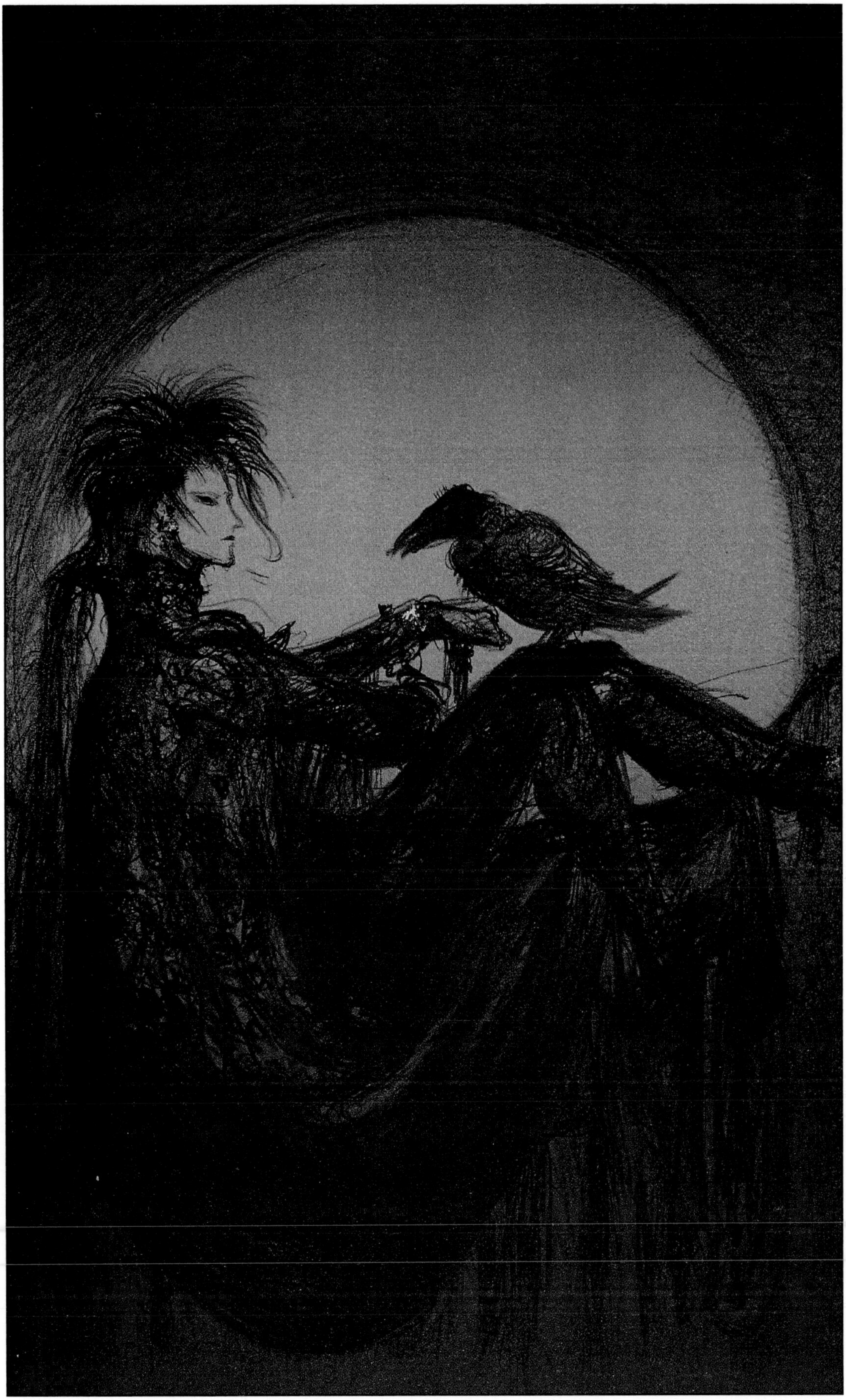

And that is the tale of the fox and the monk.

Or almost all of it. For it has been said that those who dream of the distant regions where the Baku graze have sometimes seen two figures, walking in the distance, and that these two figures were a monk and a fox, or it might be, a woman and a man.

Others say no, and that even in dreams and in death a monk and a fox are from different worlds, as they were in life, and in different worlds they will forever stay.

But dreams are strange things, and none of us but the King of All Night's Dreaming can say if they are true or not, nor of what they are able to tell any of us about the times that are still to come.

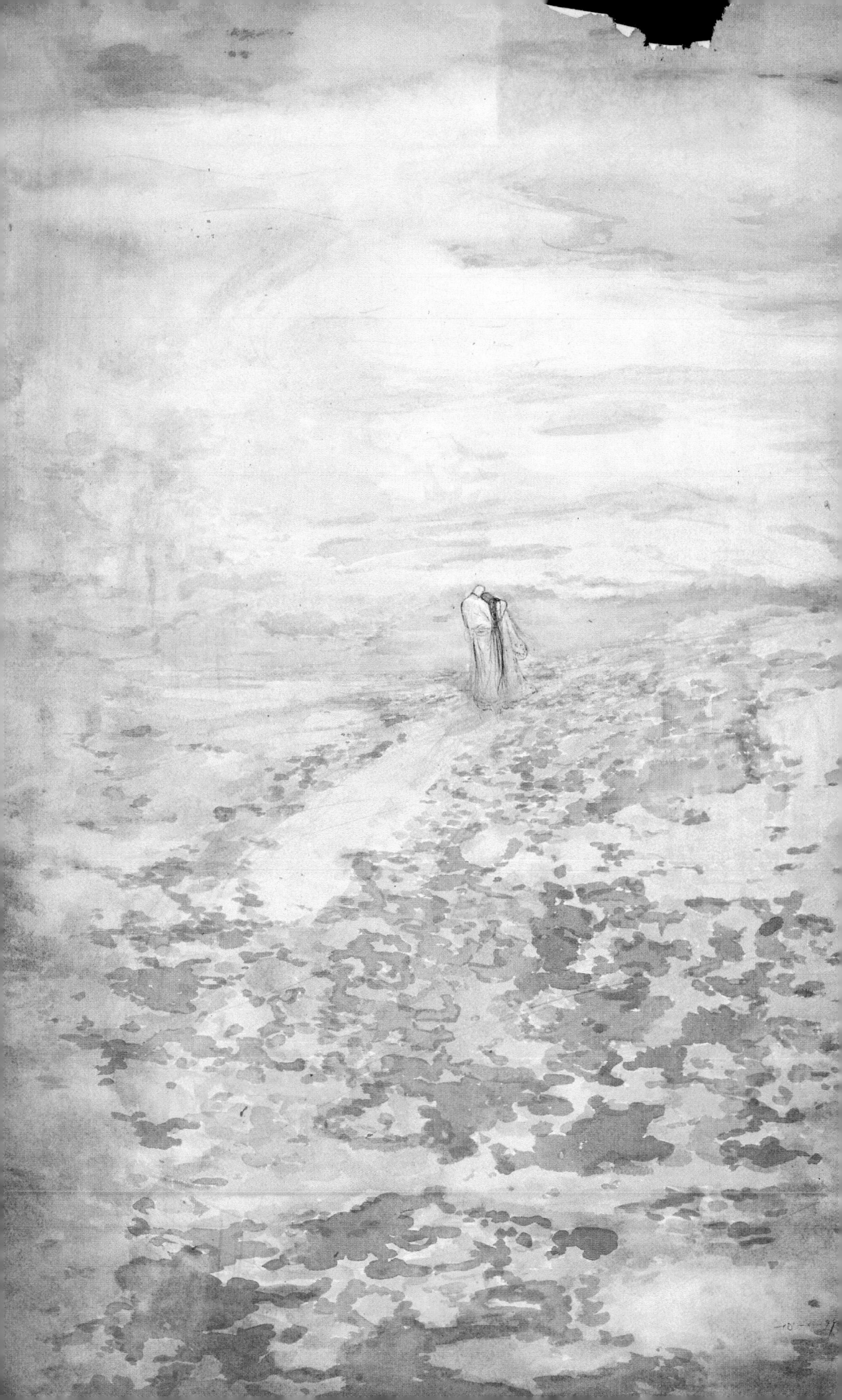

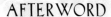

...nce to many remarkable people. Some of them will be obvious, some of them less so.

One of the least obvious people, for example, would be Harvey Weinstein of Miramax Films, for it was Harvey who asked me, over a year ago, to write the English dialogue for Hayao Miyazaki's remarkable film "Princess Mononoke."

While I was preparing for the writing process I read all the books I could lay my hands upon that dealt with Japanese history and mythology, and it was in the Rev. B. W. Ashton's *Fairy Tales of Old Japan* that I encountered the tale that Mr. Ashton called "The Fox, the Monk, and the Mikado of All Night's Dreaming" and was struck by the similarities – some of them almost disquieting – between the Japanese tale and my own SANDMAN series.

But SANDMAN was done with, and I had other tales to write, and I thought no more of it at the time.

Several months later Vertigo editor Jenny Lee was instrumental in persuading renowned Japanese artist Yoshitaka Amano to do the painting of Dream of the Endless that began the festivities celebrating the Tenth Anniversary of the first issue of THE SANDMAN.

I found his painting fascinating. I loved the perspective on the character: this was Morpheus, but a Morpheus I had never written.

Shortly after I saw the poster, Karen Berger, for the previous decade my editor on Sandman, telephoned and asked if I would be willing to write a Sandman story as a tenth anniversary project.

I asked if she would be willing to allow me to retell an old Japanese story in my own way, and she said she would.

We asked Mr. Amano if he would be interested in drawing the book. He said he would, with one reservation: while he loves comics, he does not draw them. He would, however, be delighted to illustrate it. Very well, I thought. Instead of retelling the story of "The Fox, the Monk, and the Mikado of All Night's Dreaming" as a comic, I would tell it as a longer piece of prose.

I asked Mr. Amano and his sterling lieutenants, Ann Yamamoto and Maya Shioya, to see if they could find me any other versions of the story in English translation.

The version they found for me (in photocopy form) is from one of Y.T. Ozaki's collections of Japanese tales: a strange version in which the King of Dreams is a shadowy figure, barely mentioned, who appears to be some sort of dragon, and in which the central character is the *Onmyoji*, the Master of Yin-Yang. (I am indebted to this work for much of Chapter Three, and some of the final chapter.) They also found me a Buddhist text in which the tale is alluded to, and in which the old man upon the road is explicitly identified as Binzuru Harada.

For the rest, I am indebted to the good reverend. As I write this I have my copy of *Fairy Stories of Old Japan* on the table in front of me. The leather binding is flaking and discoloured, the pages are ragged, spotted, and slightly water-stained. I felt strangely honoured to realise that, despite the battered condition of the book, I was still the first person ever to read it: many of the book's pages were still uncut. At first I cut them open with a letter-opener, then realised that they separated more easily if I simply parted them with my fingers.

I have tried to amplify, to expand and to retell the story as best I could, while taking as few liberties as possible. Most elements of the old story were close enough to their SANDMAN analogues that I would not have dared to put them in, had they not been there already: the *Itsumade* (who cried "until when?" in the boughs of a tree in the Imperial Palace) is practically a gryphon (and has almost become one in Amano-san's wonderful illustration); while the men whom the monk saw on his way to the King's house could have been, I am sure, none other than Cain and Abel; but students of folklore must simply find it in their hearts to forgive me for, at one stroke of my pen and my heart, changing Ashton's *Hototogisu* bird into a raven.

In my efforts to retell the story I made a number of errors (and in several cases, I discovered I had compounded several of Ashton's errors). Steve Alpert, from Studio Ghibli, was kind enough to catch and correct some of these, as were the people at Ten Productions. Others, I am sure, remain in the text, for the sharp-eyed to discover.

For all that is felicitous in this volume, I thank my collaborators, living and dead, and my friends.

Neil Gaiman
May 11, 1999

For me this collaboration is the first greeting between Neil and I in a relationship that will build and take many forms in the future. I was impressed by the sincerity of his attitude, and perhaps his tenacity toward his work is something that I share. It was almost destined that our paths would cross. This is only the beginning.

Yoshitaka Amano